AN INTRODUCTION TO SUNG POETRY

Harvard-Yenching Institute Monograph Series, Volume XVII

AN INTRODUCTION TO

BY KŌJIRŌ YOSHIKAWA

SUNG POETRY

Translated by
BURTON WATSON

HARVARD UNIVERSITY PRESS
Cambridge · Massachusetts 1967

TRANSLATOR'S PREFACE

Ping-tzu, first month, thirteenth day:
Timbrels beat, drums pound — Chiang-nan is falling!
Blue smoke rises under Kao-t'ing Hill.
Our ministers gape at one another like men drunk and dazed.

In the hall above, crowds of courtiers, silent, unspeaking;
General Bayan pressing for surrender papers;
Their Three Majesties together behind lowered pearl blinds;
Ten thousand cavalry, curly-bearded, circling before the palace.

(41:1a–1b)

The date indicated in the first poem above is equivalent to January 30, 1276; the place — Chiang-nan — is the region in China south of the Yangtze River — specifically, the city of Hangchow. The curly-bearded cavalry are Mongol horsemen, led by their general, Bayan; and the Three Majesties are Kung-tsung, the last emperor of the Sung dynasty (a boy of seven), and his terrified mother and grandmother. The poems are the first and third in a series of ninety-eight, written by a courtier named Wang Yüan-liang, which describe in painful detail events which he himself witnessed — the capture of the Chinese court by the Mongols and the removal of the emperor, his mother and grandmother, and his ladies-in-waiting to captivity in the Mongol capital of Ta-tu, or Khanbalik, the predecessor of present-day Peking. Some years later, the deposed emperor was allowed to become a Buddhist monk, his mother to become a nun, and the palace ladies, at the will of Khubilai Khaghan, were married off to carpenters in the suburbs of the capital. One of them, Lady Wang Ch'ing-hui, wrote of herself:

My fate was fragile as a leaf;
I wandered a road ten thousand miles.
Yellow dust here outside the Swallow Barrier;
Sad I sit and listen to the sound of cloth being fulled.

(44:3)

The ruthless sweep of the Mongol armies brought to an end what had been, culturally speaking, one of the most brilliant eras of all Chinese history, the dynasty known as the Sung, which lasted from 960 to 1279; the poems recorded above are among the last of its songs.

The West is already fairly familiar with many aspects of Sung culture. The superb Sung paintings and porcelains, those wordless works of art whose beauty may be directly and instantly perceived, have been known and admired for centuries outside of China. In recent years some of the less tangible expressions of Sung culture have also been made accessible to the West through translations and expositions: the philosophy of Neo-Confucianism, brought to fruition by Sung scholars and destined to play such an important role in the intellectual history of China, Korea, and Japan; and the religious doctrines and practices of the Ch'an, or Zen, sect, the most important sect of Buddhism in Sung times. Even a glimpse into the daily life of the Sung citizen — at least that of the city dweller — is now available to the Western reader in Jacques Gernet's *Daily Life in China on the Eve of the Mongol Invasion*.[1]

One vital branch of Sung culture, however, remains unaccountably neglected — its literature, particularly the enormous body of works written in the most important literary form of the period, the poetic form known as *shih*.

The *shih* form did not, of course, originate in the Sung; it has a very lengthy history extending back to the earliest age of Chinese poetry. Scholars generally concede that it reached its highest level of refinement during the T'ang dynasty (618–906), the great age of Chinese culture that preceded the Sung, and it is only fitting that the first studies and translations of the form in Western languages should have focused upon the masterpieces of the T'ang. The Western reader interested in

[1] Translated by H. M. Wright (New York: Macmillan, 1962). The original, in French, entitled *La Vie quotidienne en Chine, à la veille de l'invasion mongole 1250–1276*, was published by Hachetle, Paris, 1959.

the subject may turn to full-length studies of the major T'ang poets such as Tu Fu, Li Po, or Po Chü-i, or read generous samples of T'ang poetry in the versions of translators too numerous to mention.

But the greatness of T'ang poetry has for too long been allowed to overshadow the excellencies of the ages which followed, particularly those of the Sung. Sung poetry is no mere continuation of the poetry of the T'ang, but a distinct literary development, exploring directions which T'ang poetry had shunned or ignored, and striving deliberately for new effects and new values. For this reason it deserves to be studied apart from the poetry of earlier ages and to be treated to a more equitable share of attention. It is time, in other words, that the great works and writers of the Sung be made accessible to Western readers, as those of the T'ang have been in the past.

The present volume, it is hoped, will contribute to the accomplishment of this task. It is a translation of a work on Sung poetry by Dr. Yoshikawa Kōjirō, Professor of Chinese Literature at Kyoto University and one of the world's outstanding scholars in his field. The original work, entitled *Sōshi gaisetsu*, appeared in 1962 as number one in the second series of the *Chūgoku shijin senshū*, or "Selected Works of Chinese Poets" series, edited by Yoshikawa and his colleague, Professor Ogawa Tamaki, and published by Iwanami Shoten, Tokyo. The study consists of a general introduction outlining the principal characteristics of Sung poetry, followed by discussions of the most important poets of the Sung period. Numerous poems are cited throughout to illustrate the points made.

With Professor Yoshikawa's permission I have taken certain liberties in translating the book. I have added dates, explanatory phrases, and other material, where I thought they might be helpful to the reader not too familiar with Chinese and Japanese history. In other places I have made abridgments, for the following reason. When Dr. Yoshikawa quotes a poem, he accompanies the original Chinese text with a literal Japanese translation consisting mainly of a rearrangement of the Chinese characters in Japanese word-order with Japanese grammatical endings. Because this type of translation is often ambiguous even to a Japanese reader, Dr. Yoshikawa frequently follows it with notes on particular words or phrases and a paraphrase of the whole poem. When the poem is translated into English, however, the ambiguities tend —

for better or for worse! — to disappear. I have been careful to extract any important critical comments from the author's explanatory sections and to retain notes on technical terms where needed, but the paraphrases I have in most cases omitted. The author has read the translation in manuscript and has approved these adaptations of his text.

The text includes quotations of 150 complete Chinese poems, most of them of course dating from the Sung period, as well as a number of isolated lines or couplets. Naturally, in a work of this sort, many of the poems were selected by the author to illustrate certain points in his discussion and not necessarily to represent the best work of a particular poet or of the period as a whole. Some are chiefly of historical or sociological, rather than literary, interest. Others that are quite fine in Chinese do not, for one reason or another, come through very effectively in English. In a few cases I have, with Dr. Yoshikawa's permission, added a poem or two which I felt went into English better and thus might help to convey an impression of the poet's excellence.

Sung poetry — except that by writers whose whole creed was imitation of T'ang masters, dealt with only summarily in this book — is distinctive for its relaxed, more or less conversational tone, and I have aimed at a similar tone in translation. Thus the versions here, made by an American, are intended to be in colloquial American English. I am conscious that one man's colloquialism is often another man's slang or vulgarism, and I cannot expect to please all ears. It is hard enough to please one's own, even now and then. I am also aware that a single translator dealing with a variety of poets may tend to make them all sound alike, though for this shortcoming I know no remedy.

With the exception of the *tz'u* stanzas on page 8, all the poems in this volume are *shih*. Except in one or two cases the originals of these are in "lines" of a uniform number of characters throughout, either five or seven. For Professor Yoshikawa's brief discussion of the formal elements of the *shih* — brief because they had been dealt with in greater detail in a preceding volume on the T'ang period — see page 6. From that point on I have followed him in nearly always indicating the line-length of the original and the type of *shih* — "regulated verse" or "old-poetry" form — to which the quoted piece belongs.

Certain elements of the originals, such as rhyme scheme and tonal pattern, I have had to leave out of account in translation, and therefore have not indicated or discussed them. I have been careful, however, to make each line of the translation correspond to a line of the original, and the relative length of the original line is thus reflected. I am painfully aware of the disadvantages of adhering strictly to the line-for-line procedure; the five-character line goes well into English, but the seven-character line drags out to an awkward length and rhythm with the unavoidable injection of polysyllables. Nevertheless, my own experiments have not convinced me that I can make appreciable improvements by arbitrarily breaking up the lines, and so, for lack of a better solution, I adhere to the form of the Chinese. I have further attempted to reproduce, as faithfully as is consistent with English usage, the verbal parallelisms of similarity and contrast found in the originals. The alert reader will soon note, I think, that such parallelisms occur more frequently in regulated verse than in old-poetry pieces.

Professor Yoshikawa follows Chinese and Japanese custom in giving ages, according to which a person is one year old at the time of birth. Hence all ages mentioned in the text are a year above what they would be by Western-style reckoning.

I should like to take this opportunity to thank Mr. Yokoyama Hiroshi of Kyoto University for his invaluable help in compilation of the Finding List.

BURTON WATSON

CONTENTS

ILLUSTRATIONS

Imaginary portrait of Ou-yang Hsiu, after an old brush drawing. Ink rubbing of a copy engraved on stone.

Su Tung-p'o imagined on a wet day, wearing a rain hat and clogs.

Su Tung-p'o's two poems on the Spring Festival Day, in the poet's handwriting. From a collection in the Osaka City Museum.

A postscript to Su Tung-p'o's poems, composed and written by Huang T'ing-chien.

Four poems by Fan Ch'eng-ta in his own calligraphy, as engraved on stone by the monk to whom he wrote them. From an ink rubbing in the Imperial Library, Tokyo.

INTRODUCTION TO
SUNG POETRY

Chapter One

THE NATURE OF
SUNG POETRY

The Sung Period

Five great dynasties have ruled the Chinese empire over the past millenium and a half: the T'ang, the Sung, the (Mongol) Yüan, the Ming, and the (Manchu) Ch'ing. It is the second of these, founded by a Chinese family with the surname Chao, that will concern us here.

The history of this dynasty is customarily divided into two parts, the Northern Sung and the Southern Sung. The term "Northern Sung" designates the period of some one hundred sixty years (960–1126) when the dynasty, with its capital at Pien-ching — the present city of K'ai-feng in Honan province — ruled over nearly all of China. To the north lay an enemy state, the Liao kingdom of the Khitan people, which occupied the area later known as Manchuria and which, to the shame of the Sung empire, extended its domain south to include the northern parts of Shansi and Hopei provinces, the so-called "sixteen districts of Yen-yün," including the area of present-day Peking. From the middle years of the dynasty on, the Sung was also threatened by a neighbor to the west, the Hsi-hsia kingdom of the Tanguts. Within the borders of the Sung domain, however, a strong central government insured peace to China. According to a census taken around 1100 — during the reign of Hui-tsung, last Northern Sung emperor, and recorded in the "Treatise on Geography" in the official *History of the Sung* — there were 20,882,258 families in the nation, representing a population of 46,734,784 persons, while the capital city had a population of 442,940.[1]

---

[1] According to the interpretation of Prof. Miyazaki Ichisada, the second figure represents only the male population.

The prosperous and bustling life of the metropolis is described in Meng Yüan-lao's *Recollections of the Eastern Capital* (*Tung-ching meng-hua lu*, preface dated 1147). The following poem by Su Tung-p'o also indicates the flourishing of the capital and the surrounding farm region. It was written in 1093, when the poet held the post of Secretary of the Board of Rites — that is, Minister of Education. On the evening of the festival known as *Shang-yüan-chieh*, held on the fifteenth night of the first month of the lunar calendar, Emperor Chetsung, the next-to-last ruler of the Northern Sung, accompanied by his grandmother, the Empress Dowager, and the poet, ascended the palace gate and looked down over the city. On the night of the festival, which marked the first full moon of the new year, the city was lighted by thousands of lanterns; festival carts wound through the streets, and the capital was more lively than it would be on any other night of the year. The title of the poem reads: "*Shang-yüan*, attending a banquet in the tower; I showed this to my fellow officials."

> Thin snow begins to melt in fields still unplowed.
> Selling firewood, buying wine, they see the sights of peace.
> Our Prince is frugal – the clowns and mimes lack skill,
> But the year will be a good one! say laughing voices.

> (43:36/23a)

As the first line indicates, farm work for the year has not yet begun, and the capital is even livelier than usual because of the crowds of farmers who have poured in from the surrounding countryside, selling the bundles of firewood they have brought with them and using the money to buy wine, enjoying the sights of the great capital in an era of peace. The "clowns and mimes" refer to the various types of entertainers who, standing atop the festival carts, performed for the amusement of the crowd. Perhaps because the young emperor disapproves of such vain show, the entertainers this year are not as good as in the past, but this does not detract from the air of elation and confidence in what the new year will bring.

Another quatrain by Su Tung-p'o, the famous "Spring Night," may also have the capital about this time as its setting, though the date of its composition is uncertain.

Spring night – one hour worth a thousand gold coins;
Clear scent of flowers, shadowy moon.
Songs and flutes upstairs – threads of sound;
In the garden, a swing, where night is deep and still.*

(43:49–8a)

The scene is probably the poet's own house. From the second floor of a house nearby, the sound of voices and flutes performing some intricate melody drifts through the windless night. In an inner garden hangs a swing, its rope decorated with colored thread. During the day, young girls had played around it noisily, but now it hangs perfectly still, the hazy moonlight dimly lighting it.

The long Sung peace provided an opportunity for education to spread among the farming population, as may be seen from the following quatrain by one of Su Tung-p'o's disciples, Ch'ao Ch'ung-chih, entitled "Night Journey":

Old now, I care less and less about success.
On a lean horse, I travel the long road alone.
Dawn comes to the lonely village, but a lamp still burns:
I know there is a house where someone reads all night.

(10:18a)

By "success," the poet means success in the government examination, which opened the way to an official career. The poet had taken the examination a number of times in the past and had consistently failed. Seeing a light still burning in the window of the farmhouse in this isolated village, he imagines there must be some young man who, like himself in the past, had been studying all night in preparation for the examination. A poem written by Su Tung-p'o when he was exiled to the remote island of Hainan in the South China Sea indicates that, even in that out-of-the-way region, there were village schools for the education of the farm children (43:42/17a).

The 160 years of Sung peace came to an end when the state of Chin, founded by the Jurchen people of northern Manchuria, after over-

* Poems marked with an asterisk are reprinted with permission of the publisher from *Su tung p'o / Selections from a Sung Dynasty Poet*, translated and with an introduction by Burton Watson, Columbia University Press, New York and London, 1965.

throwing the Sung's old enemy, the state of Liao, launched an attack on the Sung. In 1126 the capital, Pien-ching, fell to the invaders, and Emperor Hui-tsung and his son, Emperor Ch'in-tsung, were taken prisoner and carried off to Manchuria.

Another son of Emperor Hui-tsung, who in time became Emperor Kao-tsung, fled south with a number of the officials and citizens of the capital. There he set up a new capital at Lin-an, the present city of Hangchow in Chekiang Province, from whence he ruled the area of the Yangtze Valley. This event marks the beginning of the period known as the Southern Sung. For the following century and a half, the territory of the Sung was confined to the southern half of China — the so-called "one-sided empire." To the north it confronted first the Chin state and later the Mongol hordes of Chinggis Khaghan. As in the Northern Sung period, however, the dynasty was able to maintain peace within the confines of its realm. (In this sense it differed markedly from the Japan of the same period, which was undergoing the Hogen and Heiji uprisings and the wars between the Taira and Minamoto clans.) According to a census taken in 1218, during the reign of Emperor Ning-tsung of the Southern Sung, there were 13,669,684 households in the realm. In 1276, however, the capital at Hangchow capitulated to the Mongol armies, and southern China came under the rule of the Yüan dynasty of Khubilai Khaghan. The *Meng-liang lu*, or *Millet-Dream Record*, written by Wu Tzu-mu two years before the fall of the capital, gives a detailed description of Hangchow, which overlooked beautiful West Lake with its many famous scenic spots, and was probably the largest city in the world at that time. Marco Polo, who visited the city shortly after its capture by the Mongols, recorded with admiration the wonders he saw there.

The peace that pervaded the countryside during the years of the Southern Sung is reflected to an almost tiresome degree in the huge volume of poetry — nearly ten thousand pieces — by Lu Yu, the most famous poet of those years. Let me quote one which he called "In the Village, Writing About Whatever Meets My Eye":

Rain clears from country fields – they're busy reaping wheat;
Wind is fresh in the alleyways – drying silk smells good.
People are rich in laughing words – the joy of a good harvest;

Officials reduce the tax levies – the blessing of long peace.
On branches empty of flowers, the butterfly's wings are stilled;
In woods, sweet mulberries: the oriole's throat is well oiled.
I know too well the dullness of life as a local official.
With no regrets, I turn farmer and grow old in my old village.

$$(4:16/11b)$$

The poet, who was sixty at the time he wrote this, had finished his long career as a provincial official and retired to the peaceful life of his native village in Chekiang.

To sum up, the three hundred years of the Northern and Southern Sung, though marked by struggle and defeat abroad, were years of profound peace within the borders of the Chinese empire. The power of the military class was deliberately restricted, and as a result the Chinese made a poor showing on the foreign scene, though on the other hand the nation was almost completely free of rebellion and internal strife. The *k'o-chü*, or examination system, with its preliminary examinations in the provinces and higher examinations in the capital, insured that all civil officials were chosen from among those men who had a wide knowledge of literature and philosophy. The famous historian-statesman Ou-yang Hsiu, who in 1057 acted as chairman of the examining committee for the state examination held in the capital, describes in the following lines the sound of the countless brushes of the candidates moving over their examination papers:

Warriors without a quarrel, jaws clamped bravely shut,
They move their brushes – a sound like spring silkworms munching leaves.

$$(35:12/9b)$$

One of the candidates who passed the examination on this particular occasion was the poet Su Tung-p'o.

As a result of the examination system, the men of greatest intellect and learning were often at the same time the highest officials in the government. The controversial prime minister and political reformer Wang An-shih, who was also a distinguished poet and philosopher, comes immediately to mind, but a number of the other poets who will be discussed in this book, such as Ou-yang Hsiu of the Northern Sung, Ch'en Yü-yi, Fan Ch'eng-ta, and Wen T'ien-hsiang of the Southern

Sung, all at one time held the post of prime minister, while Su Tung-p'o, the greatest of the Sung poets, though he never became prime minister, held a very important post in the government. Conversely, there are very few prime ministers or other high officials of the period who did *not* write poetry or take part in philosophical discussions. Of all the great dynasties of Chinese history, the Sung was probably the most cultured.

To be sure, the intellectual leaders of the Sung often engaged in bitter political controversies. Ou-yang Hsiu was exiled to I-ling in Hupei, and Su Tung-p'o to Hainan Island, as a result of party differences. But except in a few instances the death penalty was not customarily applied during the Sung. In this respect the Sung constitutes one of the least bloody periods in all Chinese history.

Upon this foundation of peace literature flourished, and, among the various literary genres, poetry held the place of greatest importance.

The Place of Poetry in Sung Literature

It was during the T'ang dynasty, which lasted from 618 to 907, that the verse form known as *shih*, which we shall here call simply "poetry," first became recognized as the heart of Chinese literature. The *shih*, though a very old form, underwent considerable formal development during the T'ang. The *shih* of the T'ang may be divided into two groups. First is that in the so-called *ku-shih*, or "old-poetry," form, which observes no fixed rules with regard to the number of lines or the rhyme scheme. Second is that known as *chin-t'i-shih*, or "modern style poetry," which is limited in rhyme scheme and number of lines. Poems in this latter form may be further classified into two types — *lü-shih*, or "regulated verse," which is in eight lines, uses parallelism in most of its lines, and observes elaborate rules governing tone pattern; and *chüeh-chü*, or "broken-off lines," similar to regulated verse but confined to a single quatrain. All these various verse forms became established during the T'ang as vehicles for lyric poetry; in the Sung, they were carried on and employed even more extensively than before.

One reason for this wider use was that there was a great increase in the number of men who wrote poetry. The best study we have of the lives of the Sung poets is the *Sung-shih chi-shih*, or *Notes on Sung Poetry*, compiled by the eighteenth-century scholar Li E. Counting the poets of both the Northern and Southern Sung, this work lists the names of 3,812 men. By contrast, the *Ch'üan-T'ang-shih* or *Complete T'ang Poetry*, compiled in the eighteenth century at the command of the K'ang-hsi Emperor, contains works by a little over 2200 poets. The number of poets in the Sung, if these figures are to be trusted, was almost twice as great as that in the T'ang.

Not only did the number of poets increase, but the number of poems by one man that were preserved and handed down reached staggering proportions, especially in the case of the more famous poets. We have 9200 poems from the hand of Lu Yu, the best-known poet of the Southern Sung period, and almost all of these date from the latter years of his life, when he was over forty. To mention a few other well known names, we have 2800 poems by Mei Yao-ch'en, 1400 poems by Wang An-shih, 2400 by Su Tung-p'o, 1900 by Fan Ch'eng-ta, and over 3000 by Yang Wan-li. Comparing this with the situation in the T'ang, we note that of the men who are the most prolific of the T'ang poets, there are 2800 poems by Po Chü-I, 2200 by Tu Fu, and over 1000 by Li Po; all other poets, such as Wang Wei or Han Yü, have fewer than a thousand poems to their names. Chinese scholars have compiled a *Complete T'ang Poetry*, but we do not have a *Complete Sung Poetry*. If one is ever compiled, it will probably contain several hundred thousand poems — a far greater number, certainly, than the forty thousand or so poems of the *Complete T'ang Poetry*.

Sung literature, however, does not concentrate its attention so exclusively upon poetry as did that of the T'ang. It is customary to speak of "the poetry of the T'ang and the prose of the Sung," a phrase which suggests that the heart of Sung literature is to be found in its prose rather than its poetry. This is somewhat misleading, though it is quite true that the men of the Sung expended as much care on their prose as upon their poetry, in this respect differing from the men of the T'ang. The most important development in T'ang prose had been the creation of a body of prose literature, consisting mostly of biographical pieces or essays, in the new, free style known as *ku-wen* developed by

Han Yü (768–824) and his followers. But this new prose literature had maintained a precarious and isolated existence in the midst of the flood of poetry. Toward the end of the T'ang period, its adherents had dwindled, and for a time the *ku-wen* style had passed out of existence. It remained for the men of the Sung period to revive the style and eventually make it popular. The masters of early Sung poetry such as Ou-yang Hsiu, Wang An-shih, and Su Tung-p'o, were at the same time masters of the *ku-wen* prose style. But this interest in the new prose style in no way led to a diminution of interest in poetry. As in earlier centuries, rhymed verse continued to be looked upon as the most artistic form of expression.

In addition to the *shih*, or usual poetic forms, Sung writers had at hand another genre known as the *tz'u*, a kind of song lyric composed to certain fixed melodic patterns. Unlike the *shih*, which normally employed lines composed of five or seven characters [i.e., five or seven syllables], the *tz'u* used lines of irregular length. This new form first made its appearance toward the end of the T'ang, and reached the height of its popularity in Sung times. Ou-yang Hsiu, Wang An-shih, Su Tung-p'o, Lu Yu, and most of the other Sung poets composed in the *tz'u* form, and examples are to be found in their collected works. As an illustration, let me quote a *tz'u* composed by Ou-yang Hsiu which is written to be sung to a melody entitled *T'a-so-hsing* or "Treading the Sedge." The first two lines contain four characters each, the remaining lines seven characters each; the second stanza repeats the same line pattern.

> At the lodge along the way, withered plum flowers;
> Delicate willow leaves by the valley bridge;
> Fragrant grass, warm wind that sways the traveler's reins:
> Parting grief – the farther apart, the more endless it grows,
> Long and unbroken like the river in spring.
>
> Inch on inch of gentle heart;
> Her powder-stained tears brimming over:
> The tower is high – don't go near the edge, don't lean on the railing!
> At the very end of the level plain – spring hills are there,
> But the traveler is farther away, beyond spring hills.

(35:131/9a–b)

The *tz'u* genre, as this example suggests, was originally devoted to the expression of gentle, often mildly erotic, sentiments. During the Sung, however, it grew more complex both in form and content. In addition, the Sung period saw the appearance of such men as Liu Yung and Chou Mei-ch'eng of the Northern Sung, and Hsin Ch'i-chi of the Southern Sung, who wrote exclusively in the *tz'u* genre.

The rise and spread of the *tz'u* form, because it represented a new development in the history of Chinese poetry, has been regarded as of great importance by recent literary historians. It is probable that they have in fact attached too much importance to the form. As its other name, *shih-yü*, or "remnants of *shih*," suggests, it is no more than an offshoot of the *shih* form. Although there are exceptions in the works of Sung Tung-p'o and Hsin Ch'i-chi, it is a form which, as a rule, was used almost exclusively to express minor states of emotion. As in the past, the main stream of poetic literature continued to employ the *shih* form, and the most important expressions of feeling were entrusted to this form rather than to the *tz'u*. This was the way the Sung poets themselves viewed the relative importance of the two forms, and the way in which, if we examine the facts objectively, we must view it today. Not only from the point of view of content, but from that of volume as well, we may note that the *tz'u* form falls far short of the *shih*. Although no *Complete Sung Poetry* has as yet appeared, a *Complete Sung Tz'u* has already been compiled and published.

Narrative Tendencies in Sung Poetry

Sung poetry, as we have seen, is extremely voluminous and occupies a central position in the literature of the Sung period. Though the *shih* form was already well over a thousand years old when the Sung period began, Sung poetry possesses certain characteristics which definitely set it apart from the poetry of earlier centuries and which often seem to contrast sharply with the characteristics of T'ang poetry. If we were to sum up these differences that set Sung poetry apart from the poetry which precedes it, we might say that for the men of the Sung a poem was not simply an expression of feeling, a delineation of an emotional state; it was an expression of feeling, to be sure, but at the same time it was also an expression of intellect.

First we should note the number of poems in Sung literature which are narrative in nature and are essentially expressions of intellection rather than of sentiment. Scenes and subjects which, in the literature of an earlier period, would have been treated in prose, in Sung times are frequently taken up in poetry, a process which Chinese critics have referred to as "making poetry out of prose." This tendency is already clearly discernible in the work of the Northern Sung writer Ou-yang Hsiu, who may be called the creator of the Sung poetic style. Indeed, it is perhaps because he created the style that this narrative tendency is so noticeable in his own work. It is clearly shown, for instance, in his "Song of the Japanese Sword."

This poem was written around 1060, when Emperor Jen-tsung reigned in China while in Japan Minamoto no Yoriyoshi and Abe no Sadatō were engaged in military struggle. The poet, who was a collector of antiques, had been shown a Japanese sword by a merchant from the Chekiang seacoast. The poem is in the *ku-shih*, or "old-poetry," form and is in lines of seven characters each. Because of its considerable length I shall quote it in sections.

> K'un-i is far away, unheard of any more;
> They tell a tale of jade-cutting, but who knows the truth?
> A precious sword recently has come from Japan;
> A Yüeh merchant procured it east of the spreading sea.

The name K'un-i, which appears in the *Book of Odes*, refers to an unidentified foreign land famous for its swords; legend claims that swords from this land could cut through the hardest jade. Yüeh is the old name for the coastal region in Chekiang south of the mouth of the Yangtze.

> In a scabbard of fragrant wood trimmed with fish skin,
> Yellow and white mingled in it: brass and bronze.
> A hundred gold pieces conveyed it to the collector's hand;
> He who wears it can vanquish all devilish ills.

Having introduced the sword, the poet now turns to a description of the country from which it came.

> I have heard of that country, there on a great island,
> Its soil rich, its customs good.
> Its ancestor Hsü Fu tricked the men of Ch'in;
> In search of herbs, he tarried till the boys had grown old.

In the latter years of his reign, the First Emperor of the Ch'in (r. 221–210 B.C.) was said to have sent a man named Hsü Fu, with a company of boys and girls, across the sea to search for the herbs of immortal life. According to a legend handed down in the Kii Peninsula of Central Japan, the group reached Japan, where they settled down and lived out their lives.

> With him he took the hundred craftsmen and the five grains;
> To this day, the country's crafts are marked by great skill.
> From time to time these people brought tribute to the former dynasty;
> Their scholars were often clever with verse.

Hsü Fu was said to have taken along practitioners of all the various crafts of China, as well as seeds of the five types of grain, to present as gifts to the Sea God in exchange for the herbs of immortality. The "former dynasty" refers to the T'ang, to whose court the Japanese frequently sent envoys. The poet Ou-yang Hsiu, renowned also as a historian, was the author of the *Hsin-T'ang-shu*, or *New History of the T'ang*. In that work, in his "Account of the Eastern Barbarians," he had occasion to mention the names of such famous Japanese literary figures as Abe no Nakamaro (698–770), whose Chinese name was Ch'ao Heng; Tachibana no Hayanari (d. 842), and the monk Kūkai (774–835), all of whom studied in China and were "clever with verse."

But of even greater interest to the poet is the question of whether any of the ancient classics which had been lost in China were perhaps still preserved in Japan.

> When Hsü Fu made his voyage, the *Book of Documents* had not been
>   burned,
> So the complete hundred sections must be preserved in Japan!
> But their strict laws will not allow it to be sent to China,
> Where indeed there is no one who can read the ancient texts.

The *Book of Documents*, the ancient classic of history said to have been compiled by Confucius, originally consisted of a hundred sections. But as a result of the infamous "burning of the books" conducted in the time of the First Emperor of the Ch'in, only a part of the original work remained in existence in China. Since Hsü Fu had set out on his voyage before the burning of the books took place, however, the poet surmises that the complete text of the classic must have been taken to Japan and is still preserved there. Being recognized as a work of priceless value, however, the laws of Japan prevent it from being re-exported to China. The Chinese, thus deprived of the privilege of studying the old text in its original form, have ceased to be able to read the style of characters in use in the time of Confucius.

> That a Classic of our former kings should be hidden among barbarians,
> Beyond boundless green waves where no passage lies!
> It stirs a man to feeling, it makes the tears well up –
> What heart left to talk of a little rusty sword?   (35:54/7a)

Ou-yang Hsiu's poem describing the rare Japanese sword is only one example of the numerous descriptive pieces to be found in Sung poetry. Other poems could be cited which deal with paintings, rare foods, strange animals, or unusual occurrences. Or, turning to a slightly different type of descriptive poem, we find many examples of poems which relate the experiences of a lengthy journey or the happenings of a day's outing, or describe meetings with friends, drinking parties, or other social occasions.

It is true that we may find precedents for all these types of poems in the T'ang period. Among the works of Tu Fu, for example, we have the long and masterly poem entitled "Traveling North" (Pei-cheng), which describes, section by section, the stages of a long journey. In addition, we find a number of poems by Tu Fu which describe paintings. Poems of the same type may be found among the works of Han Yü, while Po Chü-i's famous "Song of Unending Sorrow" and "Lute Song" are both long narratives relating certain historical or fictional tales. Nevertheless, it was unusual during the T'ang to write poems of this type, whereas during the Sung it became extremely common.

This phenomenon is undoubtedly related to the fact that, as I have mentioned earlier, Sung literature devoted a great deal of attention to prose. Perhaps we might say that the skill and discipline of the prose masters found their way into the realm of poetry and made it easier for Sung writers to produce long, descriptive poems of this type. But there is a more important reason, I believe, which lies deeper. The poetry of the centuries preceding the Sung, with its emphasis upon the expression of feeling, from time to time fell into a kind of vacant abstraction. There was at times a conscious disapproval of, or revulsion against, this tendency, but it was a reaction which arose spontaneously within the development of poetry itself and was not prompted by any outside influence, such as that of prose. The poets of the Sung, however, were not satisfied, as their T'ang predecessors had been, to give expression only to the most intense emotions which welled up within them. Deliberately seeking those things that would stimulate the flow of feeling, they turned their eyes to the world around them and examined it carefully. There they discovered new themes for poetry which they set about to treat in detail. And even when the themes they found were not new, their handling of them was, in that it was analytical and descriptive and did not confine itself to capturing the essence alone of the thing it dealt with. As a result, we find objects and occurrences described not only in long poems, such as that on the Japanese sword by Ou-yang Hsiu quoted above, but occasionally forming the subject of short poems in the "modern style" as well. From the enormous number of poems in the seven-character regulated verse form written by Lu Yu of the Southern Sung, let me quote an example written while he was an official in the city of Ch'eng-tu in present-day Szechwan. Describing a visit to one of the old Buddhist temples of the city, it is entitled "On Seeing the Mural in the Ch'ien-ming Temple." It was written in the autumn of 1177.

Temple built in T'ang times, set in a quiet alley,
Its famous mural neglected – half preserved, half gone.
The stirring of sparse bamboo, like endless rain;
The darkness of an old roof, making its own chill:
When I came through the gate, repeated drums sounded first call to lecture;
Now I summon my horse, slanting sun all but fills the porch.
Consider well: what appears, what fades, is surely fated:
A priceless painting left to rot here on a crumbling wall.   (4:8/11a)

The poem, it is true, ends on an emotional note as the poet ponders the sad fate of the beautiful painting, and of all things of beauty. But up to that point it is entirely devoted to a careful and evocative description of the atmosphere of the quiet temple, set far back from the busy streets of the city, and of the half-day which the poet spent there.

I have already mentioned the extremely prolific nature of the Sung poets, and this phenomenon can best be understood, I believe, if it is considered in relation to the psychology which led the Sung poets to favor descriptive poetry. When we find the majority of the poets of the age leaving behind them more than a thousand poems each, we may suppose one reason to be the fact that they are deliberately attempting to translate every sight that meets their eyes, every experience they encounter, into poetry. Needless to say, this is not the sole reason for the immense volume of their works. We should recall that frequent exchange of poems was one of the principal expressions of friendship among Chinese gentlemen; and that, as Ou-yang Hsiu mentions of his friend Mei Yao-ch'en, a man whose works were admired was often besieged by requests for poems. Nevertheless, the fact that the Sung poets did not in their later years sift through and discard any of their compositions, as most poets do, but instead carefully gathered them all together, thus producing collections of astonishing size, is surely intimately connected with the attitude of mind that seeks to treat and to capture all the manifold aspects of reality, leaving none forgotten and unsung.

The Concern for Daily Life in Sung Poetry

The eyes of the Sung men were fixed upon the world about them, and their interest was roused not only by those objects and events which might naturally be expected to make a strong impression, but often even more so by those which one might suppose would make little impression at all. They examined their daily lives and found routine details and happenings which had not been noticed by earlier poets, but which deserved to be noticed precisely because their routineness was so universal. Such mundane matters, which had not been taken up as themes in poetry earlier because they were too familiar, the Sung men proceeded with enthusiasm to treat in their poems. For this reason Sung poetry conveys the feeling of being much closer to the concerns of daily life than does the poetry of the preceding centuries.

This concern for daily life first becomes apparent in the work of Mei Yao-ch'en who, along with Ou-yang Hsiu, was one of the creators of the new style of poetry. But the same tendency is evident in the works of the poets who followed him. Let me cite an example from the works of Su Tung-p'o — a five-character "old poem" called "Children," written in 1075 when the poet was governor of Mi-chou in Shantung. The poet was thirty-nine and his two younger sons were three and five at the time.

> Children don't know what worry means!
> Stand up to go and they hang on my clothes.
> I'm about to scold them,
> But my wife eggs them on in their silliness:
> The children are silly but you're much worse!
> What good does all this worrying do?
> Stung by her words, I go back to my seat;
> She rinses a wine cup to put before me.
> How much better than Liu Ling's wife
> Grumbling at the cost of her husband's drinking! *
>
> (43:13/9a)

Liu Ling was a poet of the third century A.D. whose wife was said to have opposed his drinking.

As a further example I will quote from the works of Su Tung-p'o's political enemy, Wang An-shih. Though Wang later in life became prime minister, this poem was written when he had not yet won favor, but was still a lowly clerk in the Finance Ministry in the capital. A relative of his wife's named Wu Ch'ung had sent him a poem entitled "Thoughts on the Last Night of the Month," in which he had mentioned that he was at the moment much engrossed in the philosophy of Chuang Tzu, the Taoist mystical thinker. Wang An-shih wrote the following poem as a reply, describing the night scene in the capital in winter and his own life there. It is a five-character "old poem."

Night clouds – no sky to be seen,
Much less the stars and moon.
When the dark city dust has settled,
The boom-boom of the watch drum sounds.
Songs from an upstairs room: customers still drinking,
Drunk enough by now to be fearless of snow.
Weeping voices in the alley: other men there;
Wind from their direction brings muffled cries.
In the muddle and confusion, each man meets his fate;
Joy or sorrow – which should we prize?
Just now you are taken up with Chuang Tzu
And the wild way he throws off the bonds of the world.
Home from work, you bring out the wine,
Finger the lute strings, adjust the pick.
For myself, I sit alone doing nothing,
Facing the blue lamp that flares and fades.   (55:16/1b)

The poem quoted above describes the everyday sights and sounds of the capital. The daily life of the farmer is an even more frequent theme of Sung poetry and is dealt with in the greatest detail. The reason is probably to be found in the fact that most of the Sung poets actually came from farm villages. The most famous example that comes to mind is the poet Lu Yu of the Southern Sung, but here I shall deliberately refrain from quoting him, and shall instead give an example from the hand of Ch'in Kuan, one of the so-called "Four Great Disciples" of Su Tung-p'o. Ch'in Kuan, who lived at the end of the Northern Sung period, in the latter half of the eleventh century, came from a farming village in the district of Kao-yu in Kiangsu Province. Following is the first of a group of poems entitled "Four Poems on Country Life" in which he describes the life of his native village during the four seasons of the year. Here we see a farmer and his wife setting off at dawn for work in the fields, taking along their lunch of millet. It is a five-character old-poem.

At cock crow the whole village rouses,
Gets ready to set off for the middle fields:
Remind the wife to be sure to fix some millet,
Shout to the children to shut the gate behind us.
Spade and hoe catch the morning light;

Laughter and hubbub mingle on the road.
Puddles from the night before wet our straw sandals;
Here's a wild flower to stick in the bun of your hair!
Clear light breaks through the distant haze;
Spring skies now are fresh and gay.
Magnolia covers the wandering hills;
In the empty field, a brocaded pheasant preens.
The young people have come like racing clouds;
Owl-like, an old man squats on his heels alone.
The yellow earth glistens from the rain that passed; [2]
Clouds of dust race before the wind.
Little by little, the whole village gathers,
Calling greetings from field to field.
The omens say it will be a good month;
Let's keep on working, dawn to sundown! (25:2/4b)

This loving concern for the details of daily life is to be seen very early in the development of Chinese poetry. A large part of the three hundred poems of the *Book of Odes* deal with such themes, while T'ao Yüan-ming in the fifth century, Tu Fu in the eighth, and Po Chü-i in the ninth, have all left us descriptions in poetry of their environment and family life. But the Sung poets went even farther than these men in the degree of detail with which they depicted their everyday lives.

One of the most important causes of this tendency is probably to be found within the Sung poets themselves: the fact that, when they turned their eyes to the world about them, they looked for the most abundant reflections of reality precisely in those things that were closest and most familiar. But there is a second factor, I believe, which, if it did not actually cause the phenomenon, at least accelerated its development. It is the fact that the daily life of the Sung period and the environment in which it was lived were in many respects radically different from those of the China of pre-Sung times. They were, in fact, closer to those of modern times.

Consider this seven-character *chüeh-chü* written by Wang An-shih before he became famous, and entitled "Working for the Government."

[2] The meaning of the words *hsieh-huang,* translated here as "yellow earth," is doubtful; perhaps they connote some kind of plant.

Spring snow in Ta-liang – a cityful of mud:
Head the horse into the setting sun, ride home again.
I know what my life has been, and I can laugh –
A long long thirty-nine years of nothing!   (55:45/5a)

Ta-liang is another name for Pien-ching, the capital. The city was famous for the bad condition of its streets, which were dusty in good weather and a sea of mud when it rained. The poet, discouraged with the course of his career, coming home from the office on horseback, does not seem very different from the twentieth-century government clerk riding the streetcar home in the evening.

The pay of such a government official during the Sung — at least if he was obliged to live in the capital — was seldom large enough. Su Tung-p'o's disciple Ch'in Kuan, through the influence of his teacher, came to the capital to take a post as an editor in the court archives, but he was unable to get along on his meager stipend. He wrote the following seven-character *chüeh-chü* and sent it to the Finance Minister Ch'ien Hsieh, who happened to live in the same city block. Ch'in Kuan was over forty at the time.

Three years in the capital, sidelocks gone grey;
From old branches again I see new flowers unfold.
This daily pawning of spring clothes – it's not to buy wine;
Things are bad – at home we eat mostly gruel.   (25:10/14a)

The Finance Minister is said to have sent the poet a gift of two piculs of rice.

Men like Ch'in Kuan who journeyed from the provinces to take office in the capital had first of all to solve the problem of housing. Su Tung-p'o's cousin Wen T'ung, who was famous as a painter of bamboos, describes in a poem the troubles he encountered when he was transferred from a post in the region of what is now Szechwan to one in the capital. After much searching, he was able at last to find a house for rent in the section known as Hsi-kang, or West Knoll. The house, for which Wen T'ung paid a monthly rent of four thousand cash to the landlord, Mr. Wang, contained ten small rooms. The toilet and the kitchen were situated side by side, and by the time some beds, tables, and sofas had been put into place, there was scarcely any room left to move about.

Into this cramped area Wen T'ung and his family, ten persons in all, had to fit themselves, ducking their heads, squeezing past each other, and feeling as crowded as a snail in a shell. Summer was particularly bad, when the inside of the house was like a steam bath. With all this, however, their lot was not as difficult as that of other people, the poet tells us:

> Still we're better off than the neighbors;
> From their cold chimneys no smoke goes up at dawn.
>
> (46:18/3b)

Life in the farming villages of Sung times likewise seems to have become more complex and less primitive than earlier. Evidence of these epochal changes in the countryside is to be found not only in the poetry of Lu Yu, but in that of many other writers, forming a mine of information which students of the social and economic history of the period can ill afford to overlook. To give only one example: the Buddhist priest Ts'an-liao, who was a poetic disciple of Su Tung-p'o, in a long poem in five-character lines which he called "On the Way to Kuei-tsung," has left us a description of the farm country in Kiangsi around the foot of Mount Lu. It is evident from the poem that, just as in modern China, there were fairs held on certain fixed dates when, in stalls called *ti-tien*, sundry goods were offered to the villagers for sale.

The Sense of Social Involvement

The eyes of the Sung men were fixed upon their families and the environment immediately around them, but it was not only these things familiar and close at hand that held their interest. They also had a keen awareness of the larger units of human life, the state, and society.

This sense of social involvement — the awareness that man must live in society, that one cannot always think of oneself alone — is also a theme to which Chinese literature from earliest times has undertaken to give expression. The first examples are seen in the *Book of Odes*, while later ones are to be found in the works of Tu Fu and Po Chü-i, both men who considered themselves to be the conscience of society.

But this sense of social awareness and responsibility, though present in earlier Chinese poetry, had not yet become the universal quality it was to become during the Sung. With the Sung poets — at least the greatest of them — the quality becomes ubiquitous. It is a rare thing in the Sung to find a poet who did not write poetry of social and political criticism.

The reason for this is to be found, of course, in the fact that the humanist tradition of China, which had been fostered over so many long centuries, had entered upon a new era of growth and vitality in the Sung with the rise of the so-called Neo-Confucian philosophy. A secondary cause may perhaps be discovered in the fact that so many of the Sung poets came from the ranks of the ordinary citizenry and were therefore wholly familiar with the life of the common people. It would appear, for example, that Su Tung-p'o's immediate forebears were Szechwan cloth merchants. Such poets as he, Wang An-shih, and Ou-yang Hsiu, who came from quite modest backgrounds to pass the civil service examinations and finally to attain high office, retained a keen empathy for the common people and regarded it as a duty to work for their welfare.

Any number of examples which will serve to illustrate this point may be found among the poems quoted later on. Here let me cite a poem by Wang An-shih. Written (like the previous example from his works) before he had gained much recognition, it is a five-character old-poem called "Making Myself Get Up."

> In the cold room, wide awake and sleepless,
> I hear the noise of a cart rumbling by.
> What young boy, I wonder,
> Goes through the frosty streets before me?
> I sigh at the night not yet ended,
> Call for a lamp – "Put it there by the post."
> I push away the pillow, about to get up,
> But they tell me stars are still bright in the sky.
> The sages of old got up before dawn;
> "Cock Crow" is one of the odes of Ch'i.
> I, alas, draw pay unearned.
> I know now I've betrayed my lifelong ideals.

$$(55:16/7b)$$

At the time of writing, in the latter years of the reign of Emperor Jen-tsung (r. 1023–1063), Wang An-shih was deeply distressed by the worsening political situation. He was also busy taking care of his wife and son, who were ill, and was obliged to get up frequently in the course of the night. The poem "Cock Crow," which he refers to, is one of the odes of the state of Ch'i in the *Feng* section of the *Book of Odes*; according to the traditional interpretation, it describes an official getting up at dawn and setting off for court. Wang, hearing the sound of a one-wheeled cart, his conscience disturbed by the thought that a young boy is passing through the streets on the way to work while he himself is still in bed, ponders his failure to fulfill his duty as a conscientious servant of the people.

The Philosophical and Discursive Nature of Sung Poetry

What I have described so far may, in the terminology favored by contemporary Chinese literary historians, be labeled the realistic tendencies in Sung poetry. But the nature of Sung poetry may also be apprehended from a somewhat different angle. The Sung poets all possessed their own views of life and had a fondness for discussing their philosophies in their poetry. This characteristic is obviously related to the realistic direction which I have just mentioned. When men come to observe the realities of human life with eyes that are more closely discerning, or more widely searching, than those of the preceding ages, it is only natural that they will be impelled to give even greater thought to the question of what man is and how he ought to live. And in order to describe their philosophical observations it is natural for them to employ in their poetry the language of logical discourse, at times to the point where it seems in danger of destroying the poetic harmony of their work. Critics of the past have customarily described this as "making poetry out of argument" or "making poetry out of reason."

To understand this practice it is necessary to keep in mind that the Sung was one of the great eras in Chinese philosophy. The line of philosophical development which was carried on by Chou Tun-i and the Ch'eng brothers of the Northern Sung and reached its culmination in Chu Hsi of the Southern Sung, known in Chinese as *li-hsüeh, tao-hsüeh,* or *hsing-li-hsüeh* and referred to in English as Neo-Confucianism, sought, through the process of reinterpretation of the Confucian classics, to achieve a summation and systematization of the body of philosophical traditions handed down by the Chinese people.

The major poets of the period were sometimes on friendly terms with the philosophers, and sometimes at odds with them. Lu Yu, who was a friend of Chu Hsi, is an example of the first case; Su Tung-p'o, who made fun of the Ch'eng brothers, is an example of the second. Whichever the case might be, it was a period when poets showed a distinct fondness for philosophy and sometimes were known for their contributions to philosophy as well as to poetry. Ou-yang Hsiu, Wang An-shih, and Su Tung-p'o of the Northern Sung, and Yang Wan-li of the Southern Sung, all wrote commentaries on the classical texts of the Confucian school, and both Su Tung-p'o and his disciple Huang T'ing-chien were serious students of the Ch'an, or Zen, Sect of Buddhism.

The degree to which Su Tung-p'o, the leading poet of the Northern Sung, discussed philosophy in his poems will become apparent a little later on in the section devoted to him. Lu Yu, who holds a comparably high place in the literary history of the Southern Sung, was, if anything, somewhat reluctant to mix philosophy with poetry for fear of introducing a note of aridity. Nevertheless, he wrote the poem which I shall quote next. It was composed in 1172, when the poet was forty-seven and occupied an official position in Szechwan. In five-character old-poetry form, "The Waterfall of the Coiling Dragon" is actually a philosophy expressed in terms of water:

> From far off, tangled strands of pearl;
> Close by, a roar of tumbling thunder:
> They say the water shows its wonders
> Deliberately to startle men.
> But what does the water gain if men are startled?
> Surely it has no such thought.
> Does the water indeed have thought at all?
> It merely takes shape from the things around it.
> High up, it plunges wildly down,
> But surely it doesn't fight the rocks for joy.

T'ui-chih took a narrow view when he claimed
That all noise denotes a lack of balance.
The wise and accomplished men of old
At first wanted only to work their fields,
But someone around them roused them to act
And suddenly they found themselves doing great things.

(4:3/1b)

T'iu-chih is the polite name of the T'ang poet and Confucian philosopher Han Yü, and the reference is to his "Piece Written to Send Off Meng Chiao," in which he argues that all sounds produced by man and the natural world are evidence of a state of imbalance. This view Lu Yu rejects as far-fetched, arguing that the roar of the waterfall and the great deeds of the men of old are the result of the conditioning forces of environment.

To Lu Yu's philosophy of the water, we might compare a philosophy of the wind as expounded by Su Tung-p'o in a poem written in 1079 and describing an outing taken to look at lotus blossoms on the two rivers around the city of Hu-chou in Chekiang. It is an old-poem in five-character lines.

The clear wind – what is it?
Something to be loved, not to be named,
Moving like a prince wherever it goes;
The grass and trees whisper its praise.
This outing of ours never had a purpose;
Let the lone boat swing about as it will.
In the middle of the current, lying face up,
I greet the breeze that happens along
And lift a cup to offer to the vastness:
How pleasant – that we have no thought for each other!
Coming back through two river valleys,
Clouds and water shine in the night.*   (43:19/17a)

Expressions of philosophy are not confined to longer poems of this type, however. Even the *chüeh-chü*, the briefest of Chinese poetic forms, may convey within its four lines a philosophical idea — for example, the famous poem by Su Tung-p'o written at the time of his visit to Lu-shan, or Mount Lu, in Kiangsi in 1084 and called "Written on the Wall at West Forest Temple."

> From the side, a whole range; from the end, a single peak:
> Far, near, high, low – no two parts alike.
> Why can't I tell the true shape of Lu-shan?
> Because I myself am in the mountain.*   (43:23/6b)

Here we have the poet's epistemology expressed in terms of Mount Lu.

The Sung View of Life and the Transcendence of Sorrow

As will be apparent from what I have said thus far, Sung poetry is from the outset many-angled in its vision. On the largest scale, it reviews the problems of society as a whole; on the smallest it pries into the minutiae of everyday life. Also, as I have pointed out, it shows a fondness for philosophizing — and the fact that it attempts to apprehend and describe the nature of man and the condition of the world that surrounds him is further evidence of the broad visioned attitude that informs it. This broader vision gave birth to a new way of looking at human life, and it is this new attitude toward life which, in my opinion, constitutes the most distinctive feature of Sung poetry, the characteristic by which it differs most radically from the poetry that preceded it.

This new manner of looking at life may be described as a sublimation or transcendence of sorrow brought about through a broader and more diversified vision. It took as its initial premise the assumption that human life is not characterized by sorrow alone. In this respect it represents a complete break with the poetry of the past, which had long been accustomed to regard sorrow as the dominant quality of human life and to treat it as one of the most important themes of poetry.

Chinese poetry had for many centuries been in the habit of selecting sorrowful rather than joyful themes as the material for its lyrics. Even in the case of the *Book of Odes*, the earliest anthology of Chinese poetry compiled around 600 B.C., we find that, among the three hundred some poems, those with a sorrowful tone constitute the majority. In the age represented by the poems of the *Book of Odes*, however, a degree of optimism is still discernible in the conviction that human good will is capable by its own efforts of effecting the happiness of the individual and of society, or at least that such a capability, if not immediately realizable, is an essential part of man's nature. During the long years of the Han dynasty (202 B.C.–A.D. 220) and the centuries of political strife that followed it, however, the conviction that human existence is marked by sorrow and despair became the keynote of poetic expression. It was a conviction born of an awareness of the insignificance of man and a belief that he is wholly governed by forces beyond his control. It was further deepened by the view that despair and sorrow are burdens which man is inevitably fated to bear, and that the span of human life is no more than a brief process of decline and decay, terminating in death. It would be an exaggeration to say that all the literature and thought of this period is colored by such a view. Yet in the realm of poetry we discover it constantly in the background; and the habit of choosing despair rather than hope, unhappiness rather than happiness, sorrow rather than joy, as the theme of one's poem, became so ingrained that it was all but unbreakable.

Even the poets of the succeeding T'ang dynasty were unable to free themselves from the habit. Tu Fu regarded it as part of his duty to try to recover the optimism that had informed the *Book of Odes*, and Li Po's attitude was similar. And yet the temptation to despair continued pertinaciously to entrap even the greatest of the T'ang poets. One may say that the tension of T'ang poetry is produced by the strain of trying to discover some cause for hope in a life that seems entirely given over to despair. The men of the T'ang were aware that it was their task to try to view life as hopeful, and yet they did not live to see a time when they could do so. And the fact that they failed to accomplish the task they had set themselves may be one of the reasons for their passionate outbursts of feeling.

It remained for the poets of the Sung to complete the task. The first thing that strikes one on glancing over Sung poetry is the relatively small number of poems of sorrow. Even those poems that are predominately sorrowful manage to leave the reader with some measure of hope; they are not entirely despondent. The men of the Sung, with their diversified lines of vision, perceived clearly that human life is something more than an embodiment of sorrow. And when they had verified this perception through the agency of philosophy it became a fixed article of their faith.

This step marked a fundamental turning point in the history of Chinese literature and thought. The man who stood at the center of this change was the poet Su Tung-p'o, with his view of human life as a thing of long duration, as a process of quiet resistance. Indeed, it almost appears that his broad and forceful personality alone made the change in attitude possible. I shall discuss his role in detail in the section devoted to him later on in this book. Here I shall merely cite one poem to illustrate the new outlook which he brought to Chinese poetry.

The poem was written in 1100 when, after three years of lonely exile in the island of Hainan far to the south, the poet was at last pardoned and given permission to return to the mainland. The poet, on his way home to the north, had left T'eng-chou in Kwangsi and was traveling along the Ts'ang-wu River. The composition, in five-character old-poem form, was written for a Taoist monk named Shao and is entitled "Getting Up at Night and Looking at the Moon."

> River moon to light my mind,
> River water to wash my liver clean;
> The first like an inch-round pearl
> Fallen into this white jade cup.
> My mind, too, is like this:
> A moon that's full, a river with no waves.
> Who is it gets up to dance?
> Let's hope there are more than three of you!
> In this pestilent land south of the mountains
> Still we have the cool river moonlight,
> And I think between heaven and earth
> There are few men not calm and at peace.
> By the bedside I have wine;
> The jar brims over as though full of white dew.
> I get drunk alone, sober up alone;
> The night air is fresh and unending.
> I'll send word to the monk Shao,
> Have him bring his zither and play beneath the moon,
> And then we'll get into a little boat
> And in the night go down the Ts'ang-wu rapids.   (43:44/1b)

The lines, "Who is it gets up to dance? Let's hope there are more than three of you!" are an allusion to the poem by Li Po, "Drinking Alone under the Moon," in which the poet speaks of three companions, the moon, his shadow, and himself, drinking and dancing together.

Granted that the poet was on his way home from exile, still the trend of the political situation was difficult to predict and the future was by no means unconditionally bright for him. Yet these personal worries are for the moment cast aside while the poet sings of an optimism that overrides them. His attitude is like that of the T'ang poet Li Po, and yet his optimism is even greater. "And I think that between heaven and earth / There are few men not calm and at peace." Happiness has come to bless the entire human race. The final lines, in which the poet envisions setting out in the moonlight and descending the rapids of the Ts'ang-wu River, may be read symbolically. Su was sixty-four at the time and certainly not very strong, and yet we sense in these lines the extraordinary spirit and pluck with which he faced the future, fully intending to enjoy what was left to him of life.

Man no longer lives a petty existence, at least not petty in the degree to which it had been pictured in the poetry written from the Han to the T'ang periods. He is no longer a helpless creature pulled about by the strings of fate, plunging down a road that leads only to the grave.

This optimism is surely not wholly unrelated to the position taken by Sung philosophy. One of the objectives of the philosophers of the Sung, it appears to me, lay in the recovery of the optimism of ancient times, the optimism expressed in the Confucian classics, which speak more often of man's mission than of man's fate. The philosopher Shao Yung, who was a little older than Su Tung-p'o and who, because of his peculiar style, occupies a rather special place in the literary history of the time, consistently propounds such an optimistic view in his poetry. I shall quote an example from his collected works, a poem he entitled "Song of Perfect Peace."

> Days when the world is at peace,
> Times when life is good,
> And here we have the glory of the flowers again –
> How can you bear to go on scowling?   (57:10/148a)

Chu Hsi, the thinker who brought Sung philosophy to its highest summation, was also a poet and a first-class literary critic. In appraising the work of Tu Fu he manifested the highest respect for the great T'ang poet, but criticized Tu Fu's "Seven Songs of T'ung-ku District" for their utter immersion in sorrow. The songs, according to Chu Hsi, display a heroic strength and tension quite beyond the capacity of the ordinary T'ang poet, but their closing sections, in which the poet complains of old age and laments his humble position in life, betray an ignoble attitude and reveal the poet's failure to understand the true nature of the Way. In Chu Hsi's own words, "In these songs, Tu Fu is heroic and extraordinary in a way matched by few other poets. But a look at the final section, where he bewails old age and laments his humble station, shows a baseness of will. Can man get along without understanding the Way?" (9:84/8a) By "the Way," Chu Hsi means, it would seem, the philosophy which does not look upon human existence as petty and insignificant.

T'ang Poetry and Sung Poetry: A Contrast

The characteristics of Sung poetry which I have pointed out appear in many ways to be the direct opposite of those of T'ang poetry. This fact had already been recognized during the latter years of the Sung period itself. (See, for example, the critical remarks of Yen Yü in his *Ts'ang-lang shih-hua.*) From the succeeding Yüan period until the end of the Ch'ing in the early years of the present century, the history of Chinese poetry develops around the question of whether one ought to regard the poetry of the T'ang or that of the Sung as the standard of excellence.

The differences between T'ang and Sung poetry can probably best be illuminated through comparison. The tendency toward narrative poetry is, as I have said, rather rare in T'ang poetry, and though isolated examples of narrative poems may be found in the works of Tu Fu, Han Yü, or Po Chü-i, they are nowhere as common as in the poetry of the Sung period. On the other hand, a sense of social responsibility and involvement, which Sung poets regarded as a duty, is manifested earlier in the works of such T'ang poets as Tu Fu and Po Chü-i. Such a sense was not necessarily expected of all T'ang poets, and there are many, at least among the mediocre writers, who confined themselves to the type of poetry that the Chinese call *hua-niao-feng-yüeh* — "flower, bird, wind, and moon." Such exclusive preoccupation with nature alone was not permitted to the poets of the Sung, and as a result their poetry gives a much clearer reflection of the daily life of the period than does that of the T'ang. Though the poems of Tu Fu, Han Yü, and Po Chü-i may be said to reflect the realities of T'ang life better than those of any other poets of the period, they still tell us less about what it was like to be a member of a T'ang family, to live in a T'ang city, to work on a T'ang farm, than the works of even the minor Sung poets tell us about comparable aspects of Sung life. The poem by Ch'in Kuan describing farm life, which I quoted earlier, serves to illustrate this point, for Ch'in Kuan can hardly be called a major poet.

T'ang poetry seldom philosophizes. It is not that the T'ang poets had no philosophy. Tu Fu's famous lines, "It is easy to understand the rule of this floating world: / Prevent no creature from finding its place," (14:2499) are an expression of Tu Fu's mature philosophy, and this outlook constantly underlies his poetry. But it is rare for Tu Fu to speak of it so directly and openly, for his aim was rather that his poetry as a whole should serve as a symbol of his philosophy. The Sung poets, on the other hand, discussed philosophy directly, openly, and at great length.

In all of these ways, T'ang and Sung poetry seem to differ from each other. But there is another sense in which they are antithetical, a more subtle, and for that reason more pervading, point of difference: their approach to the problem of sorrow.

As I have explained above, the poems of the Sung men attempt to transcend sorrow. Those of the T'ang men do not; they are full of sorrow, and even a poet like Tu Fu, who tried to free himself from sorrow, could speak of "a whole life of grieving." Indeed, the minor poets of the late T'ang period seem to have regarded it as their duty to sing almost exclusively of sorrow, or rather, of despair.

One such poet was Tu Mu, whose poem, "Ninth Day," is a good example of a poem of despair. Written in seven-character regulated verse, it describes the countryside outing which was customarily held on the ninth day of the ninth month of the lunar calendar. The mountain the poet climbed on his outing was named Ch'i-shan, a small mountain in Ch'ih-chou in Anhwei, where the poet was governor at the time. Wine-drinking and the picking of chrysanthemums were by custom parts of the celebration.

> The river catches the autumn scene, wild geese begin their flight;
> My friend and I lug the wine jar and climb the blue-green hill.
> A hearty laugh is rare enough in life –
> We'll stick our hair full of chrysanthemums before we go home.
> The way to observe a fine occasion is to get quite drunk;
> No use, now we've climbed up here, to grumble at the sinking sun.
> Past and present, it has always been this way;
> Was it only on Ox Mountain that men wet their clothes with tears?
>
> (14:5966)

The last line is a reference to the story of Duke Ching (547–490 B.C.) of Ch'i who, on an outing to Ox Mountain, gazed down at his land and cities and wept, saying, "How vast! And must I leave all this and die?" (*Yen-tzu ch'un-ch'iu*, chüan 1, sec. 17.)

It would be difficult to find a poem like this one by **Tu Mu** in the corpus of Sung poetry. For the sake of comparison, let me quote a poem in the same form and dealing with the same theme by Ch'en Shih-tao, one of Su Tung-p'o's four principal disciples. Entitled "Climbing the Heights on the Ninth Day," it was written at Hsü-chou in Kiangsu, when the poet was still a student.

> Level forest, broad plain, a cavalry ground in ruins;
> A mountain temple sounds its bell, signaling dusk.
> Men will have their special thoughts today,
> Though the cold chrysanthemums smell as they did a year ago.
> My headcloth flaps up, reminding me that frost invades my hair;
> If the words are good, what harm in having a heart of stone?
> Countless falling leaves, the river that never ends –
> With this body on this day, I'm busier than ever!　(19:2/12b)

The "cavalry ground in ruins" is the so-called "Performing Horse Platform" of Hsü-chou, a site associated with the name of Hsiang Yü, a military hero of the end of the third century B.C. The sight of the ruins and the tolling of the temple bell are both reminders of the passing of time and the decay which it brings. But Ch'en Shih-tao is not, like Tu Mu, plunged into thoughts of sorrow. Men live their busy lives day by day, and each new day will bring its new thoughts and feelings — not always happy ones, but at least new ones appropriate to the new day. In this sense man is wholly unlike the chrysanthemums, which go on endlessly repeating the same cycle of growth, emitting exactly the same fragrance this year that they did the year before. Ch'en Shih-tao is here pointing to what appears to him to be evidence of the superiority of man over nature, a rather unusual view in Chinese poetry. When the T'ang poets looked about them, it was the contrast between the permanence of nature and the insignificance of man which most often struck them.

White hair, like frost, is invading his temples, but in spite of this fact, or perhaps because of it, he feels impelled to resist his environment with "a heart of stone." And the task of stringing together phrases such as "heart of stone" to form an effective poem is not unconnected with this process of resistance.

The next-to-the-last line contains an allusion to a well-known poem by Tu Fu, "Climbing the Heights," which describes the same type of outing on the ninth day of the ninth month. It concludes with the lines:

> Countless falling leaves rustle to the ground;
> The long, unending river races on its way.   (14:2467)

Tu Fu's poem describes both his sorrow at growing old in the midst of the changing universe, and the landscape which sharpens this sense of sorrow. Ch'en Shih-tao, while adapting Tu Fu's lines, has completely changed the point of view. The poet, though living in the midst of this orderly and relentless process of change in the natural world, is obliged to apply himself to the particular tasks which confront him each day, and indeed should be happy to do so. Though Ch'en Shih-tao's poem may not be completely forward-looking, it is not the poem of a man who shuts his eyes to the future. In this respect it unquestionably differs from Tu Mu's poem, which seems to have no eyes for the future whatsoever.

As suggested by Tu Mu's line — "Past and present, it has always been this way" — the wealth of sorrowful expression found in the poetry of the T'ang is a continuation of a trend already evident in the poetic works of the Han and Six Dynasties period, a keynote of sadness underlying the poetic sentiment of the time which resulted from the view of man's life as a process of headlong decline into the oblivion of death. The same sentiment is to be found in the works of the greatest T'ang masters — in these lines by Li Po, for example:

> Yesterday has gone and left me – I could not hold it back;
> Today troubles my mind – it brings greater care and grief.
>
> (14:1809)

Or Tu Fu's line:

> While I stare, this spring passes too.   (14:2475)

T'ang poetry burns with intensity. The moment in which the poem is born is one of the most vital instants in a man's life, in his headlong plunge toward death. He must fix his eyes upon the instant and pour his feelings into it. The emotion must cohere, it must jet forth, it must explode. And what he fixes his eyes upon is merely the peak, the highest point of the experience. This is how the intensity of T'ang poetry is produced; the poetry is condensed and concentrated, which means that its field of vision is narrowed.

Sung poetry is different. It looks upon life as an experience of long duration, and has a many-sided concern for this long life. It has breadth of vision, and its eyes are not riveted to the instant in which the poem is born. It does not gaze only at the peak of the experience, but examines what surrounds the peak as well. For this reason, Sung poetry is calm, even cool; or at least that is its basic tone.

It is this contrast between calmness and intensity, coolness and fire, that, more than anything else, accounts for the difference one senses when comparing T'ang and Sung poetry. As an example of the calmness of the Sung, I will quote one of the finest poems of Su Tung-p'o, the first of two written in the spring of 1082, when the poet was in exile at Huang-chou in Hupei. In five-character old poem form, it is entitled "Rain at the Time of Cold Food." The occasion known as "cold food" was marked by a feast of various foods eaten cold which came 105 days after the winter solstice and just before the Spring Festival, in the early part of April by the solar calendar. The poet was forty-six, it was his third year of exile, and life was by no means easy. Yet the tone of the poem is one of calm.

> Since I came to Huang-chou
> This is my third cold food feast.
> Each year I regret to see the spring go by,
> But it goes all the same and heeds no regrets.
> On top of that, we're pestered with rain this year;
> Two months now it's been bleak as fall.
> I lie and listen to the cherry apple flowers –
> Pale pink snow getting dirty in the mud.
> Of the forces that steal things away in the dark,
> The most powerful comes in the middle of the night,
> As though a young man were to take to his bed
> And get up to find his hair gone gray.   (43:21/25a)

The lines in which the rain carrying off the cherry apple blossoms is compared to a thief in the night are based upon a passage in *Chuang Tzu*, sec. 6: "You hide your boat in the ravine and your fish net in the swamp and tell yourself that they will be safe. But in the middle of the night a strong man shoulders them and carries them off, and in your stupidity you don't know why it happened." It is during the hours of night, when man has lost himself in sleep, that the decay which accompanies the passing of time works most effectively upon him. In the last two lines, the poet expands this philosophy to another and broader dimension through the metaphor of the youth who has gone to bed ill and, the years having raced by as he lay there, rises to find himself an old man.

This view could only be the product of an atmosphere of calm, as could the sentiment expressed earlier in the poem, "Each year I hate to see the spring go by, /But it goes all the same and heeds no regrets." At first glance the poem seems to deal with the same old theme that had occupied so many poets from Han times on and which was such a favorite in the T'ang — man and his relationship to the passing of time. And yet Su Tung-p'o has brought to the theme a new point of view which was not present in the poetry of earlier ages. Against the background of serenity he has set forth a new outlook and, on the basis of that outlook, a new philosophy.

Regret at the falling of flowers is a theme treated in T'ang times also. For the sake of comparison, I shall quote the familiar poem in five-character *chüeh-chü* form by Meng Hao-jan, called "Spring Dawn."

> Asleep in spring, unaware of dawn,
> When all around me I hear singing birds.
> Last night I heard the wind and rain,
> And flowers fell – who knows how many?
>
> (14:1667)

As T'ang poems go, this one is comparatively serene. The time span of the poem begins with the storm in the night and extends to the following dawn. But there is no philosophy, at least none that is explicitly expressed.

Or, to take the theme of regret at the passing of spring, which is also expressed in Su Tung-p'o's poem, let me quote another example from the T'ang for further comparison. This is a seven-character *chüeh-chü* by Chia Tao, "The Last Night of the Third Month," and was written to be sent to a friend.

> Third month, the thirtieth day:
> The season takes leave of a hard-working poet.
> You and I must not sleep tonight;
> Till we hear the bells of dawn, it is still spring!
>
> (14:6687)

Chia Tao was a minor poet, and the lines just quoted can hardly be said to burn with feeling. And yet the regret at the passing of spring has been concentrated in the moment of time when it is at its most intense, the last night of the season. There is nothing to compare with the broad time span of Su Tung-p'o's poem, with its mention of three springs that have passed, nor is there any impulse to examine human experience in its variety and breadth.

In comparison to Su Tung-p'o, the outstanding poet of the Northern Sung, Lu Yu, who holds a comparable place in the literary history of the Southern Sung, was more fond of passion and sorrow. He believed that the poetry of his time had gone too far in its search for calmness and its rejection of passion, and he sought consciously to correct this tendency by returning to the concentration and intensity of T'ang poetry. Yet in spite of this fact, Lu Yu's poetry differs from that of the T'ang period. Let me cite an example from his works which has a direct antecedent in the T'ang. One of six poems called "*Chüeh-chü on the Plum Flowers,*" it was written in 1202 when the poet was seventy-seven. Fang-weng is the poet's literary name.

> Plum buds have opened in the dawn wind, they tell me,
> Snow drifts that fill the hills all around.
> I wish I could change into a million selves
> So I could station one Fang-weng by every tree.   (4:50/1b)

This conceit of the poet transforming himself into a million selves is not original with Lu Yu, but is taken from a seven-character *chüeh-chü* by the T'ang poet and statesman Liu Tsung-yüan, written when he was in exile in Kwangsi.

> Mountains by the seaside – sharp pointed swords:
> When autumn comes, they stab my grieving heart everywhere.
> If I could change into a million selves
> I'd send one to climb each peak and look far off toward home.
>   (14:3931–2)

The desire to be transformed into a countless number of selves is the same with both poets. But while the T'ang poet uses the image to convey the intensity of his sadness, picturing how he would station one self upon each peak to gaze in the direction of home, the Sung poet employs it to express the serene joy of admiring the plum trees in bloom.

The Attainment of Serenity

The air of calm and serenity, as I hope I have been able to demonstrate through comparisons with the poetry of the T'ang, is a very important quality in Sung poetry, and one which the poets of the time consciously sought to attain. Mei Yao-ch'en, one of the creators of the Sung style, took as his goal what he called *p'ing-tan,* which may be rendered as "calmness" or "easiness." References to this quality are to be found in many of his poems, as, for example, in the following lines:

> In writing poetry, there is no past or present;
> The only hard thing is to be calm and easy (*p'ing-tan*).
>
> (53:46/9b)

Perhaps the best translation of *p'ing-tan* would be serenity.

This serenity in Sung poetry arose in part as a negative reaction against the passion of earlier poetry, particularly that of the T'ang, which at times became mere mannerism and struck the men of the Sung as somewhat childish. But the Sung men had a more positive aim in mind when they consciously sought to cultivate an air of serenity. They believed that in such an atmosphere the manifold aspects of human experience could be apprehended and expressed with greatest variety, precision, and detail. At least this was the aim in the case of Mei Yao-ch'en. In the grave inscription written for Mei by his friend and patron Ou-yang Hsiu, we read: "At first his work was pure, relaxed, and easy *(p'ing-tan).* After a long time, it became profound and suggestive, and at times employed clever devices to produce unusual effects" (35:33/7a). His serenity was not serenity pure and simple, but the sustaining of a kind of quiet passion. In order to store up detailed observations, passion lay concealed in the midst of serenity.

This serenity at times was carried to the point where it deprived the reader of the lyric sweetness that one customarily expects in poetry. Ou-yang Hsiu, in a five-character old poem he entitled "Sent to Tzu-mei and Sheng-yü [Mei Yao-ch'en] from my night journey to Shui-ku," describes Mei Yao-ch'en's poetry in these terms:

> Master Mei valued what is clean and succinct,
> Washing his stone teeth in the cold stream.
> He has written poetry for thirty years
> And looks on us as his juniors in school.
> His diction grows fresher and cleaner than ever;
> His thought becomes more profound with age.
> He is like a beautiful woman
> Whose charm does not fade with the years.

His recent poems are dry and hard;
Try chewing on some – a bitter mouthful!
The first reading is like eating olives,
But the longer you suck on them, the better the taste.

(35:2/5a)

This quiet passion which lurks behind the serenity of Sung poetry is one of its characteristics, and is known in Chinese as "the 'puckeriness' of Sung poetry." It is an astringent taste, not a sweet one, or at least not one that conveys the impression of sweetness.

To return once more to a comparison with T'ang poetry, we might say that T'ang poetry could be likened to wine, and Sung poetry to tea. Wine has great power to stimulate, but one cannot drink it constantly. Tea is less stimulating, bringing to the drinker a quieter pleasure, but one which can be enjoyed more continuously. And these comparisons are more than mere similes. Poems on tea-drinking first became popular with Su Tung-p'o and Lu Yu, and are seldom found in T'ang poetry. This is not to imply that the Sung men did not drink wine as well. They did, but at the same time they drank far more tea than the men of the T'ang, as pointed out by Aoki Masaru in his *Chūka chasho*, or *Tea Drinking in China*.

But the differences between T'ang and Sung are not confined to beverages, nor to poetry either; they may be seen in all aspects of the civilization of the two periods. The men of the T'ang devoted themselves to literature; those of the Sung considered philosophy as well as literature to be one of the concerns of the cultured man, a fact that did much to determine the direction which Chinese civilization as a whole was to take. Or, to turn to less broad concepts, we may note that the T'ang is famous for its multicolored pottery, while the Sung is known for its monochrome celadon or white porcelain. The architecture and gardens of the two periods likewise differed. As pointed out by the philosopher Chu Hsi, who was also a critic of Chinese civilization as a whole, the gardens and courtyards of the T'ang palaces were beautified with flowering trees and willows planted at appropriate intervals. Hence in Tu Fu's poetry we find lines such as these:

Fragrance floats through the palace – the spring wind turns;
Flowers fall on the thousand officials – the lovely scene passes.

or, "Retiring from court, they scatter beneath the flowers." But at the court of "the present dynasty," that is, the Sung, remarks Chu Hsi, "only ash and catalpa trees are planted, giving a shaded and majestic air." The remark is found in the record of Chu Hsi's conversations with his disciples, the *Chu-tzu yü-lei*, or *Classified Sayings of Master Chu*, ch. 128.

The Diction of Sung Poetry

If we leave the *tz'u* form out of consideration, we may say that the Sung simply took over and carried on the poetic forms of the T'ang. It knew no other forms than the three already developed in preceding centuries — the old poetry form, the regulated verse form, and the *chüeh-chü*. Because of its fondness for description and philosophical discussion, it preferred the old-poetry form, with its greater freedom of rhyme and length, to the more restricted form.

But though Sung poetry took over the forms of the T'ang without change, it differs from the earlier poetry in its diction and manner of expression. As with the other characteristics of Sung poetry, this can best be illustrated through comparisons with the poetry of the T'ang.

The diction of T'ang poetry is a continuation of that of the poetry of the preceding Six Dynasties period, which is noted for its elegance and floweriness. Elegance is accordingly the outstanding quality of most T'ang diction. The fact that the regulated verse form, with its elaborately prescribed technical requirements, is a product of the T'ang, brought to its highest level of development by Tu Fu, the greatest poet of the period, is proof of the prevailing concern of T'ang poetry for elegance and refinement of expression. The vocabulary of the T'ang poets, from masters like Tu Fu and Li Po down to the lesser writers, may be described on the whole as florid. The eccentricity of Han Yü's diction and the deliberate simplicity of Po Chü-i's, represent no more than isolated exceptions to this rule.

In Sung times the situation is quite different. Poetry shows a tendency to shun elegance — indeed, actually to strive for inelegance of expression. The same tendency may be seen in the choice of words;

flowery diction is rejected in favor of diction that is plain and concrete, at times so plain that, at least according to the standards of an earlier age, it might be regarded as inimical to the poetic aura of the composition. Certain words that had been used in prose, but never before in poetry, were deliberately employed by the Sung poets in their works. In doing so, they sought to arouse a feeling of resistance in the reader, and thereby to increase the impact of the poem.

Words or modes of expression of this kind are known in the language of Chinese literary criticism as *ying-yü*, or "raw words." The term was originally used by the T'ang poet Han Yü to describe the numerous examples of such "raw" or unusual diction used in his own works. During the Sung it was widely used to denote diction that conveyed a feeling of harshness or strangeness rather than gentility. Occasionally the term was given a qualifying phrase such as "raw words that blanket the sky," or "raw words stretching across the heavens." Su Tung-p'o's most eminent disciple, Huang T'ing-chien, is noted for his frequent use of "raw words," and Ou-yang Hsiu's line (in the verses quoted above) characterizing certain recent poetry as "dry and hard" is probably in the main a criticism of this type of diction.

Colloquialisms and slang are also used in poetry much more frequently in Sung times than in the T'ang. The work of the great poet of the Southern Sung, Yang Wan-li, is often cited as an example of this tendency. Colloquialisms and slang words might be expected to give an air of familiarity and ease to one's diction, and for this reason their use would appear to contradict the tendency exemplified in the use of "raw words" which startle and puzzle by their strangeness. But the contradiction is only apparent. Insofar as the use of slang words and colloquialisms represents a deliberate effort to employ words that had previously been avoided in poetry, it is in itself a type of "raw word" device. Chou Tzu-chih, in his *Chu-p'o shih-hua,* one of the numerous collections of remarks and anecdotes dealing with poetry and known as *shih-hua,* or "remarks on poetry," reports a comment which was said to have originated with Su Tung-p'o: "Everyday words, the language of the street — all can be used in poetry. The only thing that is required is skill in using them." (8:2/34)

Another factor related to diction and mode of expression is the popularity in Sung times of the practice known as *tz'u-yün* or *ho-yün*, "rhyme following," in which one composes a poem employing the same rhyme or rhyme words as those of some previous poem, usually when responding to the poem of a friend or visitor. Here, for example, is a poem written by Su Tung-p'o when he was vice governor of Hangchow. In seven-character *chüeh-chü* form, it is the third of three poems called "View from Sea Watch Tower at Evening."

> Where the green hills break, a tower of many stories:
> Those houses on the other bank – if we called, I think they'd answer.
> Autumn wind over the river, stronger by evening,
> Carries bell and drum sounds to the people of Hsi-hsing.
>
> (43:8/5b)

The tower the poet is describing stood on the bank of the Ch'ien-t'ang River which ran by Hangchow; Hsi-hsing was the ferry landing on the opposite side of the river. When Su Tung-p'o showed the poem to his younger brother Su Ch'e, the latter in response composed the following poem using the same rhyme words, *ts'eng* (stories), *ying* (answer), and *hsing* (glory).

> Towers compete for height – countless stories;
> In gentle cries the passing geese answer one another.
> A few reminders are left of the King of Ch'ien's realm,
> But that was long ago and there's no one to describe its glory.
>
> (32:4/16a)

The King of Ch'ien was the ruler who had controlled this area of China and had had his capital at Hangchow during the period of disunion that preceded the Sung.

This practice of "rhyme following," in which one takes the rhyme words of a previous poem and uses them to make a new poem, was often applied to works of considerable length in old-poetry form. If the original poem has forty lines, for example, this means that it has twenty-rhyme words, which one must use in the same order in making a new poem. The task becomes something like that of working a cross-word puzzle, and indeed the practice was naturally looked on as a kind of word game. But the nature of the Chinese language is such that it is easier than one would expect to compose poems of this type, as any one will find who tries his hand at it. Even in T'ang times, Po Chü-i and Yüan Chen had composed poems to each other's rhymes, and during the Sung it became very popular for men, as an expression of friendship, to "follow the rhymes" of each other's poems. This practice of composing more than one poem with the same rhyme words is known as *tieh-yün*, or "repetition of rhymes." Wang An-shih, struck with admiration for a poem on snow by his political rival Su Tung-p'o, wrote his own poems to the same rhymes, employing the same rhymes again and again until he had written as many as six poems on Su's original set of rhymes.

The term *tieh-yün* is also used when one uses the rhymes from one's own poems to compose a new poem. When Su Tung-p'o was confined to the Imperial Censorate Prison and was under investigation on charges of treason, he wrote a poem expressing his resignation at the thought of death, using the rhymes *ch'un* (spring), *shen* (self), *jen* (man), *shen* (spirit), and *yin* (cause). Contrary to his expectation, he was freed, and wrote a poem expressing his joy in which he employed the same rhyme words. In this case the use of the same rhyme words for poems in two such drastically different moods may also be regarded as an expression of the poet's philosophy that certain aspects of life are destined to fluctuate while others remain unchanged. The poems will be found in the section on Su Tung-p'o below.

The practice of "following the rhymes" could even be applied to the works of poets of the distant past. Su Tung-p'o is famous for having written poems to all the rhymes of T'ao Yüan-ming's poetry, though this practice was not very popular with other poets. An example of a poem by Su Tung-p'o which follows the rhymes of an earlier one by T'ao Yüan-ming will be found on page 121 below.

Another practice, though not a common one, may be mentioned here: invented in Sung times and called *chi-chü*, or "line collecting," isolated lines were taken from poems of the past, particularly those of the T'ang, and were put together to form a new poem. The statesman Wang An-shih is said to have been the inventor of this practice, which in later years was enthusiastically pursued by Wen T'ien-hsiang, the leader of the resistance movement at the end of the Southern Sung.

The collection of essays by Shen K'uo entitled *Meng-ch'i pi-t'an* records that Wang An-shih took the following lines from the works of two different early poets and put them together to form a couplet:

> The wind is still, but blossoms go on falling;
> A bird sings, making the hills seem quieter than ever.

(33:14/6a)

Wen T'ien-hsiang took lines from here and there in the poetry of Tu Fu and put them together to form new poems.

The Place of Sung in the History of Chinese Poetry

As I hope I have demonstrated above, Sung poetry represented a new departure, not only from the poetry of the T'ang, but from all the poetry of the past. Poetry that was so full of description and philosophizing, so taken up with the themes of everyday life, so socially conscious as that of the Sung, had never been known before in China. And yet in a sense the Sung merely brought to realization certain potentialities which had always existed in Chinese poetry, and which were destined at some time to be realized. The tendencies toward lengthy description and philosophizing, the concern with everyday life and social responsibility, are already apparent in the poetry of Tu Fu, Han Yü, and Po Chü-i, as I have pointed out. At first glance, Sung poetry seems to stand in contrast to T'ang poetry, and the difference is in fact a real one. And yet, in another sense, Sung poetry is a prolongation of that of the T'ang. The earliest anthology of Chinese poetry, the *Book of Odes*, is made up of two principal parts, the *Feng*, or "Airs," which are lyrical folk songs, and the *Ya*, or "Odes," which are chiefly political satires. T'ang poetry is in many respects the child of the *Feng*, while Sung poetry is the child of the *Ya*.

The Sung poets themselves were conscious of this fact. They sought among the writers of the past for those poets whom they might look upon as their literary ancestors and worked to revive their poetry, to give it the recognition it deserved, and to carry on its spirit. They looked for those qualities in the past which, though present at certain times and places, had never been dominant, and worked to make them the dominant qualities of their own time.

First of all, they sought to carry on the work of Tu Fu. During the T'ang, Tu Fu's place in Chinese literature had not yet become firmly fixed, and the situation was the same at the beginning of the Sung. It was not until the middle years of the Northern Sung and later, when the great poets of the time, such as Wang An-shih, Su Tung-p'o, Huang T'ing-chien, and Lu Yu, as literary critics extolled the work of Tu Fu, and as creative artists sought to imitate his best qualities, that Tu Fu's reputation attained the unshakable position which it holds in literary history today. In one sense the history of Sung poetry is the history of the recognition and propagation of Tu Fu's work.

Next to Tu Fu, the T'ang poets who were accorded the highest honor in Sung times were Han Yü and Po Chü-i. Han Yü, in particular, was honored for being the most consciously "unliterary" of the T'ang poets. Ou-yang Hsiu, as I shall show later in the section devoted to him, took the first step toward the creation of the new Sung style of poetry through his rediscovery and championship of Han Yü. The importance of Li Po, too, seems to have been recognized by Su Tung-p'o and Yang Wan-li, though at the moment I am unable to offer any concrete evidence.

It was not only certain T'ang poets, but on occasion poets of pre-T'ang times as well, who were rediscovered by the men of the Sung. Our present high opinion of T'ao Yüan-ming, for example, owes much to the efforts of the Sung men to revive and reappraise his work. Su Tung-p'o's role in this process was particularly important, as was that of the philosopher Chu Hsi.

In this task of reviving and carrying on the work of the great poets of earlier times, the Sung men show themselves to be heirs of the past, even in many cases the heirs of the T'ang poets, though superficially, at least, their work seems to stand in direct contrast to that of the T'ang. It was by no means only the forms of poetry that the Sung inherited from the T'ang.

In spite of this fact, however, Sung poetry is distinctly different from all the poetry that precedes it, and the difference lies in its attitude toward sorrow. The task of freeing poetry from the burden of

sorrow, a task which the men of the Han, the Six Dynasties, and the
T'ang had been unable to accomplish, and which had proved difficult
even for Tu Fu, was, under the leadership of Su Tung-p'o, finally
achieved by the Sung poets. It was this act that produced the difference.

A comparison between the poetry of Tu Fu himself and that of the
Sung poets who regarded themselves as the propagators of his methods
and ideals, will make this clear. Wang An-shih, Huang T'ing-chien,
Lu Yu — all these men sought to imitate Tu Fu's sincerity and earnest-
ness of purpose, but they by no means sought to imitate his despair.
There was a transitional period at the very beginning of the Sung, as
I shall explain a little later, which strove to imitate the grieving mood
of late T'ang poetry, and in the last years of the Southern Sung there
was once more a feeling of nostalgia for the poetry of the late T'ang
period. But this second wave of interest in late T'ang poetry sought to
recapture its delicacy, not its mood of sorrow. The tradition of the
sorrowing poet had been brought to an end in the interim.

It had been brought to an end, and was never revived in the centuries
that followed. As I have already mentioned, the poets of the Yüan,
Ming, and Ch'ing dynasties customarily chose either T'ang or Sung
poetry as the model for their own work. I hope to deal with the question
of their respective choices in a succeeding volume covering the later
history of Chinese poetry; [3] here I will only note that, generally speaking, T'ang poetry commanded greater popularity over a longer period
of time than did that of the Sung. Indeed, a reaction against Sung
poetry had already set in during the last years of the Sung period itself,
and there was a tendency to return once more to the ideals of the
T'ang. If we look for a period during which Sung poetry is admired
and imitated to the exclusion of all other poetry, we will not find it
until the latter years of the last century, when the Ch'ing dynasty was
drawing to a close. But whether the poets of the Yüan, Ming, and
Ch'ing consciously imitated the ideals of Sung poetry or rejected them,
they resembled the Sung poets in one respect, namely, that they did not
sing of sorrow, as the men of T'ang and earlier times had done. Li

---

[3] The book to which Yoshikawa refers is his *Genminshi gaisetsu* (*Introduction to
Yüan and Ming Poetry*), *Chūgoku shijin senshū* 2nd ser., no. 2, Iwanami Shoten,
Tokyo, 1963 [Tr.].

Meng-yang (1475–1531) and the others who make up the group known as the "Seven Masters of the Ming" derided the Sung poets for "making poetry out of philosophy" and reserved their admiration for T'ang poetry alone; and yet even in their poetry there is little expression of sorrow. The reason is that these men lived in an age when the preoccupation with sorrow that had become habitual in T'ang and pre-T'ang poetry had already been brought to an end by the efforts of the Sung poets.

Nature in Sung Poetry

Before bringing this introductory chapter to a close, I would like to say something about the treatment of nature in Sung poetry. Sung poetry is deeply interested in human beings, and to that extent its treatment of nature is apathetic and lacking in distinction. In earlier ages there had been poets who had made it their special task to sing of nature, particularly of its more picturesque aspects — men such as Hsieh Ling-yün in the Six Dynasties period, or Wang Wei, Meng Hao-jan, Wei Ying-wu, and Liu Tsung-yüan in the T'ang. But in the Sung we no longer find such "landscape poets."

Again in T'ang poetry, particularly in the five- or seven-character regulated verse, even when the subject of the poem is some human event or scene, it is customary to introduce the natural scene as well, depicting it either as in harmony with human emotions or at variance with them. The greater number of Tu Fu's regulated-verse poems follow this pattern. In the poem in five-character regulated verse form, "Summer-house by the River," for example, we find the lines:

> The water flows on but my mind does not race with it;
> Clouds are still, and my thoughts as slow as they.
>
> (14:2439-40)

Or in his poem in seven-character regulated verse, "Late Sunlight," the lines:

> Late sunlight enters the river, wavering over rocky scarps;
> Returning clouds veil the trees, hiding the mountain village.
>
> (14:2529)

In late T'ang poetry, this device becomes a mere mannerism, as may be seen in the lines by Tu Mu,

> Curtains and blinds of late autumn: rain on a thousand houses;
> Tower and terrace in setting sun: wind with the sound of one flute;

> (14:5964)

and in these by Hsü Hun:

> Valley clouds begin to rise, the sun sinks by the pavilion;
> Mountain rain is about to fall, wind fills the tower.

> (14:6085)

In the poetry of the Southern Sung period we find a return to this device, as I shall demonstrate later on. But in the regulated verse of the major poets of the Northern Sung it is not customary, and often all eight lines of the poem are devoted exclusively to human scenes and concerns. Mei Yao-ch'en, one of the creators of the Sung style in the Northern Sung period, boasted that in his poetry he did not, like "two or three gentlemen of the end of the T'ang," devote his energies to the depiction of the "small and trifling objects" of nature. (53:25/4b)

Another point of interest is the fact that, as Professor Ogawa Tamaki has pointed out, Sung poetry makes frequent use of personification and the pathetic fallacy, drawing nature, as it were, into the world of human activities. In his introduction to the selected poems of Su Tung-p'o in this series, Professor Ogawa cites the following example from a poem entitled "In Secretary Chang's Shou-lo Hall at Yüeh-chou":

> The green hills sprawl like a drowsy hermit
> Who most times won't go near a government office.

> (43:7/16b)

An even better-known example from the works of Su Tung-p'o is the following couplet from a poem written at West Lake in Hangchow:

> Shall I compare West Lake to the lovely Hsi-tzu,
> In light make-up or heavy, equally fine?   (43:9/6a)

Also familiar is the following couplet from a poem by Wang An-shih, one of two poems "Written on the wall of the house of the Master of Hu-yin":

> One stream guards the field, circling it with green;
> The two hills force open the door and thrust in their blue.
>
> (55:43/5a)

T'ang poetry again and again refers to two natural phenomena which inspire the feelings of the poet. One is the setting sun. For example, Tu Fu writes:

> In the setting sun my mind is still sturdy;
> In the autumn wind my illness seems to mend.
>
> (14:2523)

And Li Shang-yin writes:

> Though the setting sun is boundlessly good,
> It only draws us closer to dusk.   (14:6149)

The other phenomenon is the moon: "Thinking of home, I walk in the moonlight and stand in the clear evening" (Tu Fu) (14:2435). "The dimly shining lake does not receive the moon" (Li Shang-yin) (14: 6223).

In Sung poetry, however, these two phenomena are mentioned less frequently, it seems to me, and when they do appear, the feeling which attaches to them is somewhat different. The setting sun in Su Tung-p'o's poem, "Visiting Gold Mountain Temple," for example, inspires not sorrow but pleasure. "Mountain monks press me to stay and watch the setting sun," writes the poet. And when he consents, this is the delightful scene that he sees:

> Faint wind: on the broad water, wrinkles like creases in a shoe;
> Broken clouds: over half the sky, a red the color of fish tails.
>
> (43:7/1a)

Again, among the ten thousand poems of Lu Yu, those dealing with the moon are very few, a fact pointed out long ago by a critic of the Southern Sung, Fang Hui, in his *Ying-k'uei lü-sui* (58:22/8b).

In contrast to this, we find that the Sung poets very often mention rain. Su Tung-p'o frequently speaks of how he would like to be with his younger brother Su Ch'e, lying in beds placed side by side and talking together through a rainy night. In Lu Yu's poetry also, rain is often mentioned, and he himself gives the following advice on how to write inspired poetry:

> Shall I tell you the way to become a god in this humdrum world?
> Burn some incense and sit listening to the rain.

The setting sun is a thing that flames for a moment; the rain is a thing that continues. Again we have a hint as to how T'ang and Sung poetry differ.

Chapter Two

A TRANSITIONAL PERIOD AT THE BEGINNING OF THE NORTHERN SUNG 960–1000

Hsi-k'un Style and Imitations of Late T'ang

It was in the year 960 that Chao K'uang-yin, a divisional commander in the service of the Latter Chou dynasty, was presented with the yellow mantle of the Son of Heaven by his subordinates at a place called Ch'en-ch'iao Station north of K'ai-feng, and was persuaded to don it, thus making himself emperor of China. This event marked the beginning of the Sung dynasty, which was to last for the next three hundred years. The founding of the dynasty, however, did not mark the beginning of Sung poetry. It was not until half a century later, during the reign of the fourth Sung emperor, Jen-tsung, that Sung poetry began to assume the characteristics that would later become typical of it. During the half-century that preceded this development, not only poetry, but all Chinese literature, underwent a period of transition. During the reigns of the first three emperors, T'ai-tsu, T'ai-tsung, and Chen-tsung, the men of the time proved unable to create a new culture and civilization that would be appropriate to the new dynasty. Instead they clung, as a matter of expedience, to the remnants of the great T'ang culture that had gone before them, expending their efforts in an inept and anachronistic attempt to perpetuate forms and styles that were already dead.

I say "anachronistic" because the Sung dynasty, from its very beginning, had a different political and social organization and atmosphere from that of the T'ang. The most significant difference undoubtedly lay in the fact that, while the old aristocracy retained its importance during the T'ang, it passed entirely out of existence with the Sung. Accordingly, though it had been possible for a man during the T'ang to attain high political office through family connections alone, this ceased to be true under the Sung. Instead, we find under the Sung men like Chao P'u, the prime minister who assisted the first and second emperors in establishing the new dynasty, and who was said to have been originally the teacher of a peasant school in a farm village; or Lü Meng-cheng, prime minister in the time of the second emperor, who in his younger days was an impoverished student. In a collection of anecdotes dealing with the period, the *Ch'ing-hsiang tsa-chi,* the author Wu Ch'u-hou tells the story of how, as a young man, Lü Meng-cheng was looking longingly at the fruit peddler's melons, which he had no money to buy, when one happened to roll off into the street and he was able to snatch it up and satisfy his hunger. In the same work, Wu records the poem which Lü Meng-cheng wrote in later years to the people of his old village to tell them of his political success, which includes the lines:

> They claim that Lo-yang is full of clever fellows,
> But I say with a sigh, you'll seldom meet one like me!
>
> (5:1/2b)

In another story, Wu tells of a student named Li Hsüan who, after many bitter failures, finally passed the civil service examination in 983 and, in a poem sent to the people of his village, exclaimed:

> I write to tell my kin and friends back home:
> At last the straw hat is gone from my head!   (5:2/3a)

The "straw hat" was presumably worn by young men studying for the examination.

It was a period of transition, in many ways like that which took place in Japan at the end of the Edo period and the beginning of the Meiji Restoration. But the time had not yet come for the creation of a new culture and literature that would be worthy of the new political era.

In the world of poetry, the first half-century of the new dynasty was devoted to the emulation and continuation of T'ang styles, particularly that of the closing years of the T'ang, which, produced on the eve of the downfall of the aristocracy, was marked by sentimentality and elegance. Representative of this period in Sung poetry is the anthology in two *chüan* known as *Hsi-k'un ch'ou-ch'ang-chi,* the preface of which is dated 1104. It is a collection of 247 poems by fifteen poets who served in the government of the third ruler, Emperor Chen-tsung. Among these, the most important is Yang Yi. He and his fellow officials were assiduous imitators of late T'ang poetry, particularly the ornate and sentimental works of Li Shang-yin. Most of their works are in seven-character regulated verse. An example of a poem in this form by Yang Yi is called "Untitled." The title itself is an imitation of Li Shang-yin, who often used this designation for love poems, particularly those dealing with unhappy love. Yang Yi's poem likewise deals with the sorrow of a woman who has been cast off by her lover. The place name, "Wu-yang," recalls the tale of the goddess described in the mildly erotic *"Fu* on Kao-t'ang" by Sung Yü of the third century B.C.

> In dreams she returns to Wu-yang a thousand peaks away;
> Incense to drive off evil goes out, the kingfisher quilt is empty.
> Its shape slowly waning away – the dawn moon is mournful;
> Plantain leaves won't open to it – the spring wind is hateful.
> The darkness of distant hills: her brows forever knitted;
> Water about to overflow: her words that never come.
> Impatiently she begs the lute strings to describe her sorrow,
> Her clouds of hair, morning and night, like tumbleweed.
>
> (21:2/6a)

A reader unfamiliar with poetry of this type who comes upon this poem of Yang Yi's for the first time may perhaps mistake it for a sincere outburst of lyric sentiment. But it is in fact an exact imitation of the poetry written by Li Shang-yin some two hundred years earlier, without the slightest sign of originality. Yang Yi and his colleagues had no desire to create anything new in poetry, and, justly enough, they completely failed to do so. Their poetry is often referred to as the "Hsi-k'un" style from the title of the anthology in which it is preserved.

Other important members of the group were Liu Yün, Ting Wei, Chang Yung, and Ch'ien Wei-yen, the last a descendant of the family of kings who had ruled the area around the mouth of the Yangtze and had had their capital at Hangchow.

For the sake of comparison with the example quoted above I will quote a genuine Li Shang-yin poem, called "Untitled," in which a young official recalls a party of the evening before at which he drank and played guessing games with a beautiful young lady he had just met, before returning to his duties at the Orchid Terrace, the government archives.

> Last night's stars and planets, last night's wind,
> By the painted tower's west side, east of Cassia Hall –
> For us, no nearness of phoenixes winging side by side,
> Yet our hearts became as one, like the rhino's one-thread horn.
> From opposing seats, we played pass-the-hook; spring wine was warm.
> On rival teams, we played what's-under-it? wax candles were red.
> Then I heard the drums that called me back to work
> And raced my horse to Orchid Terrace, like tumbleweed torn loose.
>   (14:6163)

Other Minor Poets: Lin Pu (967–1028) and K'ou Chun (961–1014)

While Yang Yi and the others of his group were busy perpetuating one of the characteristics of late T'ang poetry — its preoccupation with sadness — there were other poets of this period who chose to imitate another of its aspects — the concern with a narrowly circumscribed world where one is content to live a narrowly circumscribed life. Wei Yeh (960–1019) and P'an Lang, private citizens who, unlike most of the literary men of the time, never became government officials, are examples. Wei Yeh, in a poem "Written on the Wall of a Man of Leisure, Yü Ta-chung," devised the following couplet:

> I wash the writing stone and the fish gulp ink;
> I boil tea and the stork dodges the smoke.   (51:13a)

P'an Lang, in a poem describing how he spent a summer's night at a mountain temple, employed this couplet:

The night is cool as though from rain;
The temple is silent as though there were no monks.

(24:5a)

The two couplets are prized as gems of the poetry of the period, and both show the same willingness to remain within a world of miniature preoccupations. P'an Lang, in a piece of five-character regulated verse, "On Writing Poetry," describes his own attitude toward poetic composition as follows:

> Chanting poems in a loud voice, I view a world at peace;
> It is no shame to grow old without having won success.
> Let my hairs one by one turn to white,
> Just so my poems, word for word, are pure.
> I search the end of the azure sky,
> And what I find perhaps may startle the gods.
> Beyond this I have no other thought in mind;
> The ten thousand concerns of man weigh on me lightly.

(24:6a)

The "searching" and "finding" which the poet engages in refer to the devising of quaint little couplets such as I have quoted above; beyond this, P'an Lang has no interest in anything around him. A poet's duty, it would seem, is to confine his attention to such themes as "wind, flowers, snow, and moon."

Lin Pu (967–1028), though well known in Japan from early times, is a minor poet who wrote verse of the type described by P'an Lang above. He was a recluse who remained single all his life, living on Lone Hill, a small hill situated in West Lake near the city of Hangchow. He is famous for having referred to the plum blossoms as his "wife" and the storks as his "sons." His best known works are the two poems in seven-character regulated verse titled "The Little Plum Trees in my Mountain Garden." Here I quote only the first.

Other flowers are scattered and fallen: you alone, warm and smiling,
Command all that is charming, here in the little garden.
Sparse branches slant across the clear and shallow stream;
Dark scent drifts through the dim and hazy moonlight.
Frosty birds prepare to fly down and steal a glance;

Powdery butterflies, if they knew you were here, would break their hearts.
You're in luck – here's a soft voice to coax you with songs;
No need for sandalwood clappers or wine cups of gold. (30:25b)

The "soft voice" is that of the poet himself, singing to the plum flowers and assuring them that, unlike other types of flowers, for whom elaborate feasts and entertainments are held when they are at their height, his appreciation of the plums will be a quiet and intimate affair. Ouyang Hsiu, the arbiter of literary taste in the period that followed, was said to have expressed great admiration for the couplet beginning "Sparse branches slant . . ." As a whole, however, the poem can only be characterized as fragile and lacking in power. In a sense, it is simply another expression, in a somewhat different form, of the sentimentalism of the Hsi-k'un poets.

A group of Buddist priests known as the "Nine Monks" are said to have occupied a place of some importance in the poetic world of the time, a fact which serves to emphasize how little distinguished poetry was then being written by laymen.

It is interesting to note that the preoccupation with sorrow and the narrowly circumscribed poetic world are reflected even in the poetry of the prominent statesmen of the time. The anthology known as *Erh-Li ch'ang-ho-chi*, or *Collection of Poems Exchanged by the Two Lis* (preface dated 993), which was long ago lost in China but preserved in Japan, is, as its title indicates, a collection of poems exchanged by two friends, Li Fang, high minister to the second Sung ruler, Emperor T'ai-tsung, and Li Chih, another high official of the time. The collection, which contains 123 poems, is characterized mainly by poems of a delicate and somewhat erotic nature, much like those of the Hsi-k'un anthology compiled a few years later.

The outstanding statesman of this period was K'ou Chun (961–1014). Prime minister to Emperor Chen-tsung, he played an important part in the military and diplomatic relations with the Liao state, the Sung's enemy to the north, and in his private life was said to have imitated the extravagant ways of the great T'ang officials. Contrary to what one might expect from his position and manner of life, however, his poems are often expressions of private sorrow, as, for example, the following seven-character *chüeh-chü*, called "Spring South of the Yangtze."

> Dim and distant, misty waves keep us a thousand miles apart.
> The scent of white duckweed scatters when east wind comes.
> The sun sets behind the islands, and as I gaze,
> Sorrowful thoughts, like the spring river, never end.

$$(15:1/29a)$$

Or, to quote another example, a poem in five-character regulated verse entitled "Climbing a Tower on a Spring Day and Thinking of Going Home":

> A high tower broadens the view a little:
> Dark, dark – the plain with a single river.
> A country watercourse where no one crosses,
> The lone boat all day lies on its side.
> From the deserted village come ragged mists;
> In an ancient temple, swooping orioles chatter.
> My old home is a long way beyond the clear Wei –
> Lost in thought, I suddenly awake with a start.

$$(15:2/34a)$$

The writer was a native of the region of Hsia-kuei in Shensi, and hence speaks of his home as being far beyond the Wei River that runs through western Shensi. The couplet beginning "A country watercourse" has been much admired. As one may see, the poem deals with private thoughts and feelings. In addition, according to the collection of essays entitled *Hsiang-shan yeh-lu* by the monk Wen-ying, the poet's contemporaries considered it too melancholy an outburst for one who occupied the position of prime minister (22:1/12).

If the life of a prime minister was not really a cause for such sadness, then why did K'ou Chun write poems like these? He did so, I believe, because the old view, which held that one must somehow or other inject a note of sadness into one's poems, still commanded adherence. During late T'ang times and the period of disunion and military strife which followed, when men of the educated class were looked down upon and no one who was capable of writing poetry was likely to succeed in the world, it was not inappropriate for poets to hold such a pessimistic view and to express their grief and frustration in their works. But under the Sung, the situation had changed, and men of learning who in earlier times might have ended their lives in obscurity were now occupying important posts in the government. And yet when they came to write poetry, they continued to follow the literary convention of a bygone age. Thus we have the appearance of such anomalous figures as K'ou Chun, the lamenting prime minister.

Wang Yü-ch'eng (954–1001)

But even while outmoded conventions continued to prevail, there were signs of the impending birth of a new kind of literature. Yang Yi, for example, did not write only of sorrowful love as in the lines quoted above. He also wrote poems with such titles as "The Prisons are Full of Convicts," or "Many of the People's Oxen are Dying of Plague," which foreshadow the concern for political and social problems that was to become such a prominent mark of the poetry of the following period.

The name of Wang Yü-ch'eng is often mentioned as one of the forerunners of the new movement in Sung poetry. Wang Yü-ch'eng was born in 954, six years before the founding of the Sung, the son of a miller in Chü-yeh in Shantung. His literary talent won recognition from the local authorities, and early in the reign of the second ruler, Emperor T'ai-tsung, at the age of twenty-eight, he passed the civil service examination and received the *chin-shih* degree. In later years he alternated between provincial posts and posts connected with literary activities in the central government. He died in 1001, early in the reign of Emperor Chen-tsung. In his career, he is typical of the members of the new Sung bureaucracy; but his poetry is totally unlike that in the Hsi-k'un style which dominated the literary world of his time.

First we may note that, of the poets of the past, Wang Yü-ch'eng admired the most philosophical of the T'ang poets, Li Po, Po Chü-i, and particularly Tu Fu; in this respect his attiutde is atypical of his time. During the Five Dynasties and early Sung, the poetry of Tu Fu was more often viewed with indifference, and Yang Yi, the leader of the Hsi-k'un group, had a distinct dislike for it, referring to Tu Fu as "the village gentleman." In the works of Wang Yü-ch'eng, by contrast, we find such lines as "Tzu-mei's [Tu Fu's] collected works open the world of poetry!" (23:9/15b) or "I am one who follows after Lo-t'ien [Po Chü-i]; I wonder if I dare take Tzu-mei as my predecessor?" (23: 9/15b), which indicate the admiration he had for Tu Fu and Po Chü-i. Related to this preference in poetry was his admiration for the T'ang prose of Han Yü and Liu Tsung-yüan, creators of the relatively free style known as *ku-wen* in reaction against the ornateness and artificiality of "parallel prose." Most of Wang Yü-ch'eng's contemporaries, when writing prose, still employed the parallel style. In a poem presented to his friend Chu Yen, he remarked: "How wonderful, that you share the same likes with me/The prose of Han and Liu, the poems of Li and Tu" (23:10/19a). In another poem, he speaks of "examining the *ku-wen* of Han and Liu" at the same time that he mentions "taking up the works of Li and Tu" (23:3/4b).

Probably as a result of these tastes, Wang Yü-ch'eng's collection of poems, the *Hsiao-ch'u-chi*, contains a number of rather long narrative poems, and is also rich in works which display a concern for political and social problems, both characteristics of the poetry of the age that was to follow, but exceptional in Wang's own time. In a long five-character poem entitled "Pity for the Refugees," (23:3/9a) he tells how one winter day when he was an official in Shang-chou in Honan and was dozing in the sun on the porch of the official lodging, he was informed that a peasant family consisting of an old man and woman, their son, and three grandchildren, driven abroad in search of food by the famine in Shensi, had stopped to rest in front of his gate. After learning their story and relating it in detail, the poet ends with the reflection that he himself is no more than a "stealer of food," a recipient of a stipend which he does not deserve. The poem, forty-four lines long, with a total of 220 characters, is rare in early Sung poetry both for its length and its subject. Because it is so long, however, I shall not quote it here, but give instead another of his poems. This one is in seven-character regulated verse and is called "Journey to a Village."

> My horse threads a mountain trail through bamboos just yellowing;
> I let him go the long road – the country holds my eye.
> Countless valleys, taking voice, fill with echoes of evening;

A few peaks, speechless, stand in the slanting sun.
Leaves fall from the quince tree, the color of rouge;
Buckwheat flowers open – fragrant white snow.
What's this? My poem done, I'm suddenly lost in thought;
This village bridge, those meadow trees are like the ones at home!

(23:9/11b)

It is probable that the poem was written when the poet was on his way to one of the provincial posts to which he was assigned, a form of demotion when he had fallen out of favor in the capital. The first part of the poem seems conventional enough, and yet the poet has in certain respects opened new ground not explored up to this time. The lines "Countless valleys . . ." and "A few peaks . . . ," are early usages of the pathetic fallacy, a device which was to become so common in later Sung poetry. Again, the buckwheat flowers, though not entirely unmentioned in earlier poetry, are rather novel in feeling.[1] In the last couplet, the image of the poet "lost in thought" is conventional enough, but the content of his thought is not. While earlier poets would almost certainly have remarked that the bridge and the trees before them were *not* like the ones at home, and would have become lost in thought at that melancholy fact, Wang Yü-ch'eng reports the exact opposite, thus suggesting that his thoughts may not be entirely unhappy ones.

The thirty *chüan* of the *Hsiao-ch'u-chi*, which represent the complete works of Wang Yü-ch'eng, contain four *chüan* of old poetry, five *chüan* of poems in regulated-verse form, and two *chüan* of poems in a ballad form known as *ko-hsing* — a total of about five hundred poems. Not only are Wang's poems unusually numerous, but they provide material upon which a detailed biography of the poet could be constructed. Both facts — their number and their biographical nature — ally them more closely with the works of the great Sung poets who followed than to those of the T'ang poets.

The *Hsiao-ch'u-chi* bears a preface written by the poet and dated the last day of the twelfth month of the third year of *Hsien-p'ing*, a date that would fall early in 1001, about a year before his death. It

---

[1] For an earlier use of this image, cf. Po Chü-i: "The buckwheat-flowers, in the light of the moon, shine white as snow" — in "The Village at Night," as translated by Arthur Waley in *The Life and Times of Po Chü-i* (London, 1949), pp. 79f [Tr.].

is quite possible that the work was printed not long after its completion. We know, for example, that the thirty-*chüan* collected works of Hsü Hsüan, a poet slightly older than Wang Yü-ch'eng, were printed as early as 1016. From earliest times, up through the T'ang, books were disseminated in handwritten copies, but from the Northern Sung — or, to be more exact, from the very end of the T'ang and the succeeding Five Dynasties era — the art of printing came into use. The new invention was both the cause and the result of an increased number of readers and symbolized the beginning of a new epoch in the dissemination of literature. Sung literature was probably urged forward in the new direction it had begun to take by this purely mechanical factor as well as by the other factors I have already mentioned.

One more indication of the formation of a new literary taste may be pointed out. Anthologies, through their manner of selection, represent a type of literary criticism. Among the anthologies which date from this period is the *T'ang-wen-ts'ui*, or *Masterpieces of T'ang Literature*, in 100 *chüan* — an anothology of T'ang prose and poetry compiled by Yao Hsüan and completed in 1011, which, incidentally, served as the model for the early Japanese anthology of works in Chinese by Japanese writers, the *Honchō monzui*, or *Masterpieces of Our Country*. In compiling his work Yao Hsüan deliberately avoided highly elegant works, stating in his preface that he had selected mainly works "of old style correctness" and shunned those marked by "extravagant language and florid diction." In his selection he has included only poems in old-poetry form, and none in the regulated verse form. This was done partly as a reaction against an earlier anthology, the *Wen-yüan ying-hua*, or *Blossoms of the Literary Garden*, in 1000 *chüan*, compiled during the *Hsiung-hsi* era (984–987), which had selected mainly works of T'ang literature noted for their elegance of style and form. The Japanese anthology already mentioned, *Honchō monzui*, though it borrowed its title from the *T'ang-wen-ts'ui*, included only the most florid and elegant works of the Heian period *kambun* writers. In this sense, it completely missed the spirit of the Chinese work it was imitating.

Chapter Three

THE MIDDLE PERIOD OF THE

NORTHERN SUNG

1000 — 1050

Ou-yang Hsiu (1007–1072)

It was during the long, forty-two-year reign of Jen-tsung, the fourth of the Sung emperors, over half a century after the founding of the dynasty, that the men of the Northern Sung first became truly aware of the fact that they were living in a new era, for which a new style of poetry was appropriate and desirable. Thus the reign of Jen-tsung, which lasted from 1022 to 1063, marks an important period in the history of Chinese poetry.

The new movement in Sung poetry centered about two close friends, Ou-yang Hsiu and Mei Yao-ch'en. Of the two, Mei was the better poet, though Ou-yang exerted a greater influence on the age. The latter made highly significant contributions to Chinese culture not only in the field of poetry, but in that of prose, historiography, classical studies, and archeology as well, and, through the breadth of his talents, in time attained the highest political post in the government, that of prime minister. As such, he became in effect not only the political, but the cultural leader of the nation as well, a fact which explains why his influence was so much more pervasive than that of Mei Yao-ch'en.

The reign of Jen-tsung marked a turning point not only in the history of poetry, but in the whole cultural growth of China. For it was during this period that the ancient Confucian philosophy, after many centuries of relative neglect, was once more recognized as the proper ethical guide of the Chinese people, and the application of its teachings became one of the most important duties of the individual and of society as a whole. Putting into practice the political principles of Confucian philosophy meant insuring that the government was in the hands of men of learning and moral perception, an ideal which was realized through the examination system. As a result, the political leaders of the nation became identical with its cultural leaders. Such famous statesmen as Fan Chung-yen, Fu Pi, Wen Yen-po, and Han Ch'i, representatives of the new bureaucracy drawn from the intellectual class, were charged with the political and cultural leadership of the nation. Ou-yang Hsiu was one of this group.

These men, surveying the past of China, looked upon the culture and civilization of the Six Dynasties and T'ang periods, when the supremacy of Confucian teachings had been successfully challenged by Buddhism and Taoism, as decadent, and declared their intention of shaking off its influence. At the same time they rejected the highly ornate literature typical of these periods on the grounds that it, too, was decadent and lacking in thought, and worked instead to create for their own age a literature with greater philosophic depth and content. Emperor Chen-tsung, the ruler who preceded Emperor Jen-tsung, had been infatuated with the superstition-ridden teachings of Taoism, and the poetic world of his time, as I have already mentioned, was dominated by the florid Hsi-k'un style, facts which served only to add impetus to their desire for a radical change.

Emperor Jen-tsung was a weak ruler, constantly embroiled in harem troubles, but he was not a tyrant. On the foreign front, the Sung still faced its old enemy, the Liao state, to the north, while beyond the western border a new threat appeared in the form of the Hsi-hsia state, established by the Tangut people. To each of these states the Sung yearly sent a huge tribute, known as a *sui-pi*, or "annual gift," by which it bought immunity from attack. It was the resulting era of peace that made possible the new cultural developments referred to above. The changes which took place at this time were in many respects to decide the shape of Chinese civilization for the next thousand years, until the final overthrow of the imperial system in 1911. From this period on, the authority of the Confucian doctrine remained unchallenged, and Buddhism and Taoism declined in importance. Similarly, in the field of letters the literary ideals established in the time of Emperor Jen-tsung remained in large part the ideals of Chinese literature until the present century. Prose writers of later centuries looked upon Ou-yang Hsiu as their finest model, and his influence remained unabated until the rise of the *pai-hua*, or colloquial style movement, in the twentieth century.

The reign of Emperor Jen-tsung, then, represents one of the most important eras in Chinese history. Its influence reached even to Japan, for the Confucianism which was introduced to Japan in the Edo period and which became such an important factor in Japanese life and thought, derived essentially from this period, and held up the culture and civilization of this period as its ideal. The *Ming-ch'en yen-hsing-lu*, or *Record of the Words and Deeds of Eminent Statesmen*, an account of the careers and sayings of the famous officials of the time of Emperor Jen-tsung, was required reading for our forefathers in Japan until recent times. Japanese writers of the Edo period who wished to learn to write Chinese prose customarily took as their model the works of Ou-yang Hsiu. Among the various eras into which the reign of Emperor Jen-tsung is divided, that known by the name *Ch'ing-li*, which lasted from 1041 to 1048, is remembered in particular, both in China and Japan, as a time of cultural brilliance.

Ou-yang Hsiu was one of the leaders of this period of brilliance and innovation, particularly of its literary aspects. The son of an impoverished provincial official, he was born in 1007, seventeen years before Emperor Jen-tsung came to the throne. His father died when he was four, leaving him to the care of an uncle. There was no money to buy writing materials for the boy, and it is said that he learned characters by watching his mother trace them in the sand with a reed. He himself has recorded that his literary awakening came at the age of ten when he happened to discover an incomplete copy of the collected works of the T'ang poet and prose master, Han Yü, in the library of a wealthy family in the neighborhood. The writings of Han Yü, as I have already noted, are the least ornate and flowery of all T'ang works, and in the time of Ou-yang Hsiu's youth, when the Hsi-k'un style was at the height of its popularity, they were almost wholly neglected. The fact that Han Yü's writings happened to come into Ou-yang Hsiu's hands so early in his life no doubt had much to do with his later decision to take Han Yü as his model both in prose and in poetry.

In 1030, when he was twenty-four years old, Ou-yang Hsiu came out first in the civil service examination held that year and entered upon a career as a government official. During the long years of Emperor Jen-tsung's reign that followed, his fame as a scholar and intellectual leader steadily grew, and his position in the government became progressively high. His career suffered two setbacks, however, when he came into conflict with the conservative faction within the government.

The first of these setbacks occurred in 1036, when Ou-yang Hsiu was thirty, and was brought about because he opposed the banishment of Fan Chung-yen, a leader of the reform faction to which Ou-yang Hsiu belonged. As a result, Ou-yang Hsiu was transferred to the post of district magistrate of Yi-ling, the present-day Yi-ch'ang in Hupei, a demotion that amounted to exile. The event is the subject of a poem entitled "Four Worthy Men and One Unworthy One" by Ou-yang Hsiu's friend Ts'ai Hsiang, which laments the fall from power of Fan Chung-yen, Ou-yang Hsiu, and the others of their group. Seven years later a shift in the political situation allowed Ou-yang Hsiu to return to the capital and, along with such men as Tu Yen, Fan Chung-yen, Fu Pi, and Han Ch'i, to resume a position of importance in the government. A poem written in 1043 by his friend Shih Chieh and called "Poem of the Sagely Virtue of the Ch'ing-li Era" praises the statesmen of this period.

Ou-yang Hsiu's second setback came when he was shifted to the post of governor of Ch'u-chou in Anhwei because he had incited too much opposition at court. This second reverse, however, merely had the effect of increasing the fame of Ou-yang Hsiu and his associates. In the latter years of Emperor Jen-tsung's reign, the position of Ou-yang and his party became firmly established when he was appointed Ts'an-chih-cheng-shih, or prime minister, one of the highest posts in the government. When death brought Jen-tsung's long reign to a close in 1063, Ou-yang Hsiu was fifty-seven. Testamentary instructions of Emperor Jen-tsung ordered Ou-yang Hsiu and Han Ch'i to assist Emperor Ying-tsung, his sickly successor, and they guided the state through the period of struggle and instability which ensued. In addition to such duties, Ou-yang Hsiu from time to time acted as chairman of the examining committee which administered the chin-shih examinations. By custom the students who passed the examination looked upon the chairman of the committee as their teacher, and in this way many of the brightest young men of the period, such as Su Tung-p'o, became Ou-yang Hsiu's disciples. Thus his position as cultural leader of the nation became more firmly established than ever.

The complete writings of Ou-yang Hsiu were compiled by his son Ou-yang Fei and his disciple Su Tung-p'o. Of the 153 *chüan* which make up the work, twenty-three are devoted to poetry; these contain 359 poems in old-poetry form, and 470 in regulated verse and *chüeh-chü* form, arranged more or less in chronological order.

There are, on the whole, two distinctive qualities which mark the poetry of Ou-yang Hsiu. First is its serenity — a serenity which is not simply a reflection of negative resignation, but which has a positive and conscious objective — emancipation from the preoccupation with sorrow. This preoccupation, which marred so much of T'ang poetry, was, as I have said, uncritically accepted and imitated in the early years of the Sung. It was this obsessive melancholy of the T'ang and early Sung that Ou-yang Hsiu rejected; and in a larger sense he rejected the whole burden of sorrow which had weighed upon Chinese poetry from the Han and Six Dynasties. His way of doing so was to make himself the imitator, not only as a prose writer but as a poet as well, of Han Yü, the man whose works he had discovered with such excitement in his youth. Han Yü's poetry contains less of the melancholy element than that of any other T'ang poet, a fact which I have already pointed out in my post-script to the selection of Han Yü's poems in this series. In the poetry of Han Yü's literary successor, Ou-yang Hsiu, sorrow is even more rigidly restrained.

The second quality to be noted in Ou-yang Hsiu's poetry is its liberality of outlook, a quality which becomes possible to the mind that has succeeded in restraining the irritability of grief. The quality is to be seen first of all in a broadening of subject matter. As I mentioned earlier, when quoting Ou-yang Hsiu's poem on the Japanese sword, poems describing antiques or household objects are already to be found in T'ang poetry. Han Yü, for example, tried his hand at the genre, as in his "Song of the Stone Drums" and similar pieces. But Ou-yang Hsiu went much farther in this direction than Han Yü. Not only in pieces describing antiques, but in other types of descriptive poems, Ou-yang

Imaginary portrait of Ou-yang Hsiu, after an old brush drawing.
Ink rubbing of a copy engraved on stone.

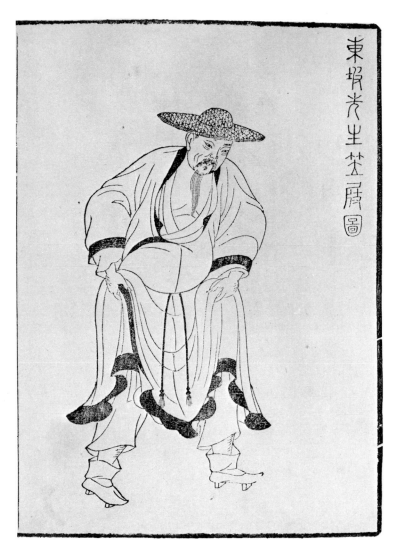

Su Tung-p'o imagined on a wet day, wearing a rain hat and clogs.

Hsiu sought for a broader selection and treatment of themes, as I shall
have occasion to mention later.

His breadth of outlook is reflected not only in his search for a wider
variety of themes. Even when he took up a subject that had been dealt
with many times before, he somehow broadened it in treatment and
often accompanied it with philosophical comment. In a word, it was
Ou-yang Hsiu who laid the groundwork for the typical Sung poetry
which I have described in the Introduction. To read his poems in
chronological order is to see the process by which this groundwork was
laid. It is to watch not only the maturing of a single artist, but the
growth of a whole new poetic style.

Ou-yang Hsiu's fondness for descriptive verse is evident even in
his early works. In 1033, for example, when he was twenty-seven and
serving as a local official in Loyang, he was obliged by government
business to make a trip to the capital, Pien-ching. The poem which he
wrote describing the journey, entitled "In Place of a Letter" (35:2/5b),
consists of 56 lines, or 280 characters. It records various incidents that
occurred along the way, such as falling in with the funeral of a wealthy
family and being roundly snubbed, and reads with all the interest of
a travel diary.

In the early volumes of his poetry, one still encounters a certain
number of songs of sorrow, particularly among the works written
during the period of his second exile to the provinces. Here is an
example, a seven-character *chüeh-chü*, which dates, however, not from
his second period of exile but from his first. As he was on his way up
the Yangtze to his new post in Yi-ling, his boat tied up at Chiang-chou,
the place where the T'ang poet Po Chü-i, here referred to as Lo-t'ien,
had been banished centuries before.

> Lo-t'ien once was exiled to this river shore,
> Sighed to the far horizon and wept his tears.
> Today for the first time I know how great my fault:
> Yi-ling is three thousand li beyond here!   (35:56/6a)

Ou-yang Hsiu has left us a description of Yi-ling in his prose piece,
"Record of the Chih-hsi Hall of Yi-ling-hsien" (35:39/2a). The district
was situated 5,590 li from the capital, at the place where the Yangtze

emerges from the Three Gorges and begins to flow less turbulently. The region produced pepper, lacquer, paper, and other products. The marketplace, says Ou-yang Hsiu, stank of half-rotten fish and shellfish, and beneath their crude roofs of bamboo and rushes, the local inhabitants shared their huts with pigs. Tile roofs were considered unlucky, and for this reason the villages of the region often suffered from disastrous fires. In a seven-character poem in an expanded form of regulated verse [1] which he sent to his friend Mei Yao-ch'en, Ou-yang Hsiu gives a skillful description of the local customs, with their round of religious observances and mingling of non-Chinese elements. While expressing the poet's loneliness and discomfort, it is not an unrelieved lament of despair, and the light note upon which it ends shows the effort of the poet to put a restraint upon sorrow.

> Green hills each way I look, jumbled and without end;
> Chickens, dogs; bleak and lonely, a few hundred houses:
> By Ch'u custom, the seasons are full of spirit festivals.
> The language of barbarian hamlets makes no sense to a Chinese.
> So swift the river where it skirts the city, boats can hardly anchor;
> So high the mountains facing the town, the sun sets early.
> Beating drums, stamping and singing, they hold night fairs;
> Catching turtles, divining for rain, they rush to burn off the fields.
> In the thick woods, weird birds fly even in daytime;
> By garden edges, I see strange flowers blooming out of season.
> But the river and the mountains are beautiful beyond compare!
> If I could get someone to paint them, you'd see why I boast.
>
> (35:11/4a)

The place of his second exile, Ch'u-chou in Anhwei, was likewise situated in a remote and mountainous region where both the scenery and the way of life were monotonous. Shortly after his arrival, his daughter died. As he observes in a five-character old poem written at this time: "White hair: My Daughter Shih Died," this was the third time he had lost a daughter.

> Though my years number less than forty,
> Three times I've broken my heart mourning a child.
> The pain of it once is too much to bear –

[1] Three quatrains instead of the usual two [Tr.].

Who can stand it again and again?
Pain in my heart spreads to my mind,
My mind crumbles – the ache is in my bones.
Blood seeps from my mind and bones
And overflows in streams of bright tears,
Tears that go on until the blood is gone;
My hair and skin grow chill and lightless.
So it is natural my hair and beard
Should turn gray before I am really old.   (35:2/12a)

On such an occasion it is understandable for any poet to give himself up without restraint to the expression of grief, and Ou-yang Hsiu is certainly no exception. And yet one should note the curiously logical way in which the spread of grief from one part of the body to another has been treated, each step in the development being represented as the result of the step before.

Here is another piece written during the same period of exile, a five-character old poem named "Thoughts on the End of Spring."

I have no way to drive off deep sorrow;
Spring days are quiet, growing longer.
Fragrant wind enters the heart of the flowers;
Flowering branches at midday bob up and down.
Back and forth the bee picks among the blossoms;
His comb is not yet filled with clear honey.
Spring nights are most beautiful now;
Fallen petals one by one whirl through the air.
Yellow butterflies, nothing else to do,
Fly here and there to help them in their hurry.
Singing birds change their tune from time to time,
New notes skillfully blown from their flutes.
Spider webs are the idlest of all,
Their sunny light dangling a hundred feet.
The Heavenly Craftsman tends to creation's changes;
The ten thousand things respond to spring sun.
I alone don't know what the season is,
I've lain here ill so long in the empty hall.
Seasons pass and I cannot hold them back.
My unfolding songs of themselves grow sad.   (35:2/8a)

The poem begins with a sorrow that refuses to be driven away, and ends with the bed-ridden poet sighing at the passing of the seasons. In this respect it is simply a continuation of the theme of the shortness of man's life that was so often treated by the poets of the Six Dynasties and the T'ang. But the poet's real efforts, one feels, were expended upon the description of the harmony and activity of nature that occupies the central section of the poem. The beauty of the spring scene depicted there almost seems capable of absorbing and canceling out the melancholy which precedes and follows it. In this sense the poem is the exact opposite of those of earlier ages, which start out with the objective of escaping sorrow and fleeing to brighter moods but end by being enveloped in it.

It was around this time that Ou-yang Hsiu, with a certain degree of irony, adopted the literary name Tsui-weng, or Drunken Old Man, though he had just turned forty. To celebrate the occasion, a monk friend named Chih-hsien had a little pavilion built for him at Mount Lang-ya called Pavilion of the Drunken Old Man. The following five-character old poem entitled "Written for the Pavilion of the Drunken Old Man at Ch'u-chou," more clearly than ever conveys the poet's determination not to lose himself in melancholy.

> Forty – that's not so old!
> Drunken Old Man just happens to be a name I have.
> In drunkenness I forget all things –
> How then can I keep track of my age?
> I love the water below the pavilion
> That comes from between jumbled peaks,
> Its voice seeming to fall from the sky,
> Pouring toward the gap between the eaves,
> Flowing into the cliff-bound valley
> To feed the bubbling of hidden springs.
> Its roar doesn't drown out human voices;
> Its clear tone is not that of flutes and strings.
> Not that I don't love pipe and string,
> But musical instruments are too much bother.
> So from time to time I take some wine
> And walk the long way to these swirling waters.
> Wild birds eye my drunkenness,

Valley clouds keep me from waking.
Mountain flowers know how to laugh
Though they haven't learned to talk with me yet.
And then the wind comes from the cliffs
To blow me back to sobriety again.   (35:53/13b)

Another poem written in 1043, the third year of Ou-yang Hsiu's exile in Ch'u-chou, shows this tendency even more clearly. In seven-character old-poem form, it is called "Drinking a Little at the Pavilion of Rich Happiness."

The Creator, feelingless, has no preferences;
Spring colors come to the deep hills too.
Mountain peach, valley apricot – not much to see,
Yet, true to the season, they open in the spring wind.
The strolling girls, come to look, don't understand ugliness;
Their old fashioned make-up and country ways match the red of the flowers.
The joy in life consists in savoring things.
While there's wine, don't turn your back on the gem-green cup.
And you, host! don't make fun of the flowers and girls!
What are you anyway? An old man facing flowers.   (35:3/10a)

The "host" is the poet himself. An old man, he may not be the most appropriate person to join a group of young girls and beautiful flowers. Yet, since what joy there is in life lies in accepting and savoring the lot assigned to one, it behooves the poet to accept the fact that he is an old man facing flowers, to recognize the limitations of such an existence, but at the same time to make the most of it.

In the late years of Emperor Jen-tsung's reign, when Ou-yang Hsiu was growing old and his position as a leading statesman had become firmly established, his poetry became increasingly serene in feeling. And, from the security of this calmness, his lively intellect sought in all directions for new themes to treat in poetry. Themes which the poets of the past, in their preoccupation with sorrow, had not attempted to treat — indeed, would have been ashamed to treat — were taken up by Ou-yang Hsiu at this time. In addition, Ou-yang Hsiu, a master of prose style, made a conscious attempt to transfer to the medium of poetry the skill which he had learned in prose, working to make his descriptive passages freer than ever. Among his works of this period are to be found many poems describing in detail his associations with Mei Yao-ch'en, who was an official in the capital at this time, and other friends, or dealing with aspects of his family life. Other poems deal with foods or beverages such as tea, crabs, or ginko nuts. Because he was a collector of antiques, many poems deal with that subject, such as the "Song of the Japanese Sword" already quoted. Finally, as befits his high position in the government, there are many poems on political themes.

As an example of this last type, I shall quote a seven-character old-poem entitled "The Dreg-eaters." Wine-making had from early times been a government monopoly in China. It was the duty of the farmers to grow the grain from which it was made, but the wine itself was sold by the government at far too high a price for the ordinary farmer to be able to afford. In place of wine, the farmers found themselves having to buy the lees, or dregs, which remained after the wine had been brewed, in order to have something to eat. The injustice of the situation disturbed Ou-yang Hsiu, and he believed that it was the duty of the officials to take steps to remedy it.

Farmers grow the grain, officials brew the wine;
You pay a tax even on the pint or gallon.
Wine sells for cash, but dregs are discarded;
In the big breweries they pile up each year till they rot.
The wine, still working, foams like boiling water;
East wind comes to blow me the fragrance of the vats.
Rows and rows of jars and pots –
Just so I can get a taste!
What the officials sell is rich and good; in the villages, it's thin;
He who drinks official wine every day is surely happy.
But haven't you seen, in the fields, the people planting grain?
In their kettles no gruel to get them through winter and spring;
So they come again to the officials to buy dregs to eat,
And the officials dole them out "as a special favor!"
Ah – these officials of ours,
Whose job it is to "head" the people –
They are clothed without raising silkworms, eat without plowing;
All their study is "righteousness and benevolence."

Benevolence means caring for people, righteousness is doing what's right,
Speaking words that carry through, using strength where it will help.
But they look up and cannot aid the welfare of the state,
Look down and cannot feed the starving people!
I drink wine,
You eat dregs —
Even though you don't accuse me,
How can I escape the blame?   (35:4/9a)

Another piece, "Calligraphy Practice," the second of two with that title in five-character old-poem form, sets forth the poet's philosophy in terms of an event in his daily home life.

> Practicing calligraphy, I didn't know night had come;
> I only wondered why the west window had grow so dark.
> My tired eyes already were bleary;
> I couldn't tell if the ink was thick or thin.
> All man's life has this same unawareness —
> He works and works, not really minding,
> When all he gets is an empty name,
> A thing that shines the space of an hour.
> There's a truth here not confined to calligraphy practice;
> Let me make it into a motto for future warning!   (35:4/9a)

Ou-yang Hsiu served as prime minister during the brief four-year reign of Emperor Jen-tsung's adopted son and successor, Emperor Ying-tsung. In 1071, the fourth year of the reign of the next ruler, Emperor Shen-tsung, he retired to a country home in Ying-chou in Anhwei Province which he had purchased earlier. The following year, at the age of sixty-six, he died. It was just at this time that Wang An-shih, one of Ou-yang Hsiu's juniors in the government and a man in whom he had placed great hope, betrayed Ou-yang's expectations and began putting through the violent reform program known as the "New Laws."

Ou-yang Hsiu's poetry is neither as minute in description as that of his friend Mei Yao-ch'en, nor as broad and profound as that of the man who turned against him, Wang An-shih. The fact that as a critic of poetry he showed such a great fondness for Han Yü and little for Tu Fu, that he ranked Li Po as a greater poet than Tu Fu, revealed defects of judgment not typical of his customary enlightenment. His opinion on the latter point is to be found in the piece entitled "Discussion of the Relative Merits of Li Po and Tu Fu" in his collection of essays, the *Pi-shuo*, in which he writes: "Tu Fu was able to rival only one aspect of Li Po's art. He surpassed Li Po in effort and stamina, but he could not match the way in which Li Po gave free rein to his genius." (35:129/3a)

Yet, as I have said before, it was Ou-yang Hsiu who laid the foundation for the many-sided vision which was to mark the new style of Sung poetry. The following five-character *chüeh-chü* may be said to symbolize his approach to poetry. It is entitled "Distant Mountains."

> Mountain colors, be they near or far –
> I watch the mountains, walking all day.
> Sharp peaks, round crests shift with every angle;
> A stranger walks by, ignorant of their names.

(35:10/9b)

Mei Yao-ch'en (1002–1060)

Ou-yang Hsiu laid the foundation for the new style of Sung poetry. But as a high official he was busy with state affairs, and as a leading prose writer he was occupied with the task of creating a new mode of expression based upon the so-called *ku-wen* style created by Han Yü, with its freedom of rhythm, but modified in the direction of greater smoothness of expression. Ou-yang Hsiu's two great historical works, the *Hsin-T'ang-shu*, or *New History of the T'ang*, and the *Hsin-Wu-tai-shih*, or *New History of the Five Dynasties*, took up much of his time, together with his works on the *Book of Changes* and the *Book of Odes*, and his collection of ancient stone inscriptions, the *Chi-ku-lu*. As this list of activities indicates, Ou-yang Hsiu played the part of leader in many different phases of the new cultural development, and for this reason it was difficult for him to devote all of his energies to poetry alone. The task of perfecting the new poetic style which he had created was left to two of his friends who were free to concentrate upon the writing of poetry, Mei Yao-ch'en and Su Shun-ch'in.

Mei Yao-ch'en was a native of Hsüan-ch'eng in Anhwei Province.

He was born in 1002, five years before Ou-yang Hsiu. The two men first became acquainted in the early years of Emperor Jen-tsung's reign, when, both of them around thirty, they were assigned to posts in Loyang, the so-called Western Capital. At that time, Mei Yao-ch'en had already received warm praise for his poetry from his official superior, Wang Shu, who declared that "for the past two hundred years there have been no such works as these!" (35:42/11b) His poetry made an even more profound impression upon his fellow official, Ou-yang Hsiu. The friendship they formed at that time continued throughout their lives, until 1060, when Mei, at the age of fifty-nine, succumbed to the plague that swept the capital that year. At that time Ou-yang Hsiu held the post of prime minister, while Mei Yao-ch'en was only a minor official in the Ministry of Justice, and the other families living in the narrow alley around Mei's rented house no doubt stared in wonder when the carriage of the great statesman pulled up before Mei's door and Ou-yang Hsiu entered to pay his condolences. The poems which the two men exchanged in the course of their friendship are recorded in great number in their collected works. Ou-yang Hsiu invariably expressed the highest admiration for Mei's poetry. The poem quoted earlier, in which he compares Mei's poems to olives that become more flavorful the longer one chews on them, is only one example of his praise.

Mei responded to the encouragement of his friend and devoted all his energies to poetry. As an official, he made such poor progress that his wife was led to remark ruefully that he was like a catfish trying to climb a bamboo pole, but his lack of worldly success only inspired him to expend great effort on poetry. Ou-yang Hsiu, in the preface he wrote to the collected poems of Mei Yao-ch'en, remarks, "It is not that poetry makes paupers of men, but that in most cases men must first become paupers before they can write good poetry." (35:127/9a) And in an elegy written on Mei's death by a man who was much his junior, Wang An-shih, Wang remarks on the fact that Mei continued to work at his poetry up to the very end of his life. "Most men are keen enough in their early years but lose their keenness with age"; writes Wang An-shih; "he alone continued to labor away without ever stopping" (55: 13/4a).

As I have mentioned in my Introduction, Mei Yao-ch'en took as the slogan for his poetry the term *p'ing-tan* — "calmness" or "ease." But this "ease" of his seems to have been a quality attained only after a period of friction. Far from being calm by nature, Mei was a man of keen and delicate nerves, and often gave expression to a mood of uneasy sadness, as in the following five-character regulated poem he called "Hearing the Wild Goose."

> Damp clouds do not scatter even at night,
> Though their thin places dimly show the stars.
> The lone wild goose – how fast he goes!
> His single cry saddens me, but I listen for it again.
> In his heart he must be missing old companions;
> He has already climbed high into the deep blue,
> And after so many days over hills and lakes
> He'll join the ducks and seagulls that crowd the shore.
>
> (53:10/16a)

This impression of delicate sensitivity is further strengthened if we examine the "Three Poems Lamenting the Dead" and other works which he wrote after the loss of his first wife and in which he describes in great detail his feelings at that time. I shall quote one of these, the third of the "Three Poems Lamenting the Dead," which is in five-character old-poetry form.

> The long-lived and the short-lived there have always been.
> How would I dare challenge the azure sky?
> Yet of all the wives of the world I've seen,
> None were like her in beauty and worth.
> If the stupid alone are granted long life,
> Still could she not have been *lent* a few years?
> And I watched while my jewel worth a string of cities
> Sank out of sight in the nine-leveled springs.[2]   (53:10/16a)

But Mei Yao-ch'en realized that a new era in poetry could not be created by sentiment alone, no matter how keen and delicate the nerves that express it. He believed that poetry should not be left to the

---

[2] As the sky is imagined to consist of nine levels, so the land of death, known in Chinese as the Yellow Springs, is here pictured as being nine levels in depth [Tr.].

domination of sentiment, but that a new type of poetry should be created through the introduction of reason and intellect. In a poem written in reply to his friend P'ei Yü, he stated this himself. Paraphrased for the sake of clarity, this is what he said: You think it peculiar that I should devote myself entirely to poetry and not take up any other kind of writing. But I am not writing poetry for no reason at all. Worthless as my poems may be, they are composed with great effort and care. I am striving to follow the *Ta-ya* and *Hsiao-ya* sections of the *Book of Odes* (that is, to write poetry of social criticism). I have no intention, he added, of spending all my time fashioning miniature scenes and landscapes like some of the poets in the latter days of the T'ang (53:25/4b).

In this same poem he describes himself as negligent in other types of writing, though as a matter of fact he wrote commentaries on the military classic *Sun Tzu*, and on the *Book of Odes* (which he did not live to complete), and works on the history of the T'ang period, so he can hardly be called negligent. In view of this breadth of interests, it is easy to see why he found it difficult to fix his eyes only upon the realm of sentiment. As Ou-yang Hsiu says in the grave inscription which he wrote for his friend: "He was not stubborn and narrow-visioned like some of the men of the T'ang who called themselves poets" (35:33/8a).

Sustained by his keen sensitivity, Mei Yao-ch'en turned his eyes in all directions. As his allusion to the *Book of Odes* mentioned above would suggest, he very often made political and social problems the concern of his poetry. Examples are to be seen in his three poems, "Poverty Along the Canal," "The Tale of the Farmers," or "The Poor Girl of Ju-fen," all of which describe the sufferings of the common people and express indirect criticism of the government. His poem "On hearing that a holder of the *chin-shih* degree is selling tea" is an attack on corruption among the intellectual class and provides a valuable insight into the social history of the period.

The broadening of vision and subject matter which characterizes the poetry of Mei Yao-ch'en not only led him to take up themes that were larger than those of his predecessors, but some that were more minute. Here, for example, is a poem which he wrote on the subject of lice. That he was consciously attempting to write on the smallest subject imaginable is indicated by the title of the poem, which states, "Shih-hou pointed out to me that from ancient times there had never been a poem on the subject of lice, and urged me to try writing one." Shih-hou was Hsieh Ching-ch'u, a nephew of the poet's first wife.

> A poor man's clothes – ragged and easy to get dirty,
> Easy to get dirty and hard to keep free of lice.
> Between the belt and the lower robe is where they swarm,
> Ascending in files to the fur collar's margin.
> They hide so cleverly, how can I ferret them out?
> Dining on blood and making themselves at home —
> My world too has its sallies and withdrawals;
> Why should I bother to pry into yours?   (53:24/10a)

The outstanding characteristic of Mei's work is this desire to broaden the subject matter and scope of poetry, to turn the keen eye of his poetry upon the scenes of family life and of his associations with his friends, and to examine such scenes more deeply and in greater detail than any of the poets before him had done. As examples, let me quote two poems dealing with night scenes. The first, a five-character old-poem entitled "Aboard a boat at night, drinking with my wife," was written when the poet and his second wife were en route by boat from the capital to his post in the provinces.

> The moon appears from the mouth of the sheer bluff,
> Its light shining behind the boat over there.
> I sit drinking alone with my wife;
> How much better than facing some dreary stranger!
> The moonlight slowly spreads over our mat,
> Dark shadows bit by bit receding.
> What need is there to fetch a torch?
> We've joy enough in this light alone.   (53:28/13b)

The second is a five-character old-poem "At night, hearing someone singing in the house next door." The fourth line is an allusion to the story of a famous singer of ancient times whose voice was so beautiful that the very dust on the rafters stirred in response.

Midnight, but I still haven't gotten to sleep
When I hear faint sounds of singing next door.
I picture to myself the red lips moving;
The dust stirs from the rafters, I know.
She makes a mistake and laughs to herself.
I get up to listen and put on my robe;
Put on my robe, but the song has ended.
The moon in the window shines a little while more.

(53:31/3a)

Other examples of the poet's interest in heretofore overlooked themes may be found in the poem called "The Lice in Hsiu-shu's Head," which describes the poet's feelings as he picks lice out of the head of the son left him by his deceased wife; or the one entitled "My neighbor to the south, Secretary Hsiao, comes to visit in the evening," which tells how a minor official in the neighborhood, whom the poet had hardly known previously, came to announce that he was being transferred to another post; the poem celebrates the new friendship which the two men struck up as a result of the visit. Both these poems deal with themes that, in the literature of the present day, would probably be treated in the autobiographical novel. Or, taking particular lines in Mei's poetry, one could mention the following: "In the solitary bed, all alone, my knees begin to jiggle" (53:18/6a), which refers to the kind of nervous quivering or jiggling of the legs known in Japanese as *binbōyusuri,* or "poor man's shake"; or this line: "The foolish boy imitates the crying of a cat" (53:11/9b), a description of a child making cat-like noises in the hope of frightening away the rats. Both lines represent the kind of minute observation that is not to be seen in the works of earlier poets.

Looking at those poems which deal with themes outside the poet's family life, we may mention the one which describes Chin-ming-ch'ih, or Gold Bright Lake, a pleasure park in Pien-ching (K'ai-feng) (53:32/5a); the poem describing how Mei, along with his friends Liu Ch'ang and Chiang Hsiu-fu, visited the temple called Hsiang-kuo-ssu to look at paintings by Wu Tao-tzu and terra cotta statuary by Yang Hui-chih (53:38/10b); or that telling how he bought ink from an old man at one of the many open air stalls lined up beneath the cedar trees around the temple (53:17/10a). He wrote poems dealing with the seller of plum flowers, the sellers of leeks, smartweed, and other vegetables; poems on the gift of ice which Ou-yang Hsiu sent him during the hot weather (53:21/4a); or on the gift of ginger pickled in wine lees given him by Liu Ch'ang (53:50/9b). He wrote a poem to apologize for the time when Ou-yang Hsiu, Wang Chu, Han Chiang, and Wu Kuei all came in a group to see him when he was not at home (53:50/10b), and another one relating how he went to visit Fan Chen and, finding him out, left his card and returned home, only to discover that Fan Chen had been to his own house during his absence (53:58/1b). Though I have mentioned here only a few of the types of themes which are to be found among Mei's poems, it is apparent with what thoroughness they reflect the realities of life in the capital in the early half of the eleventh century.

Mei Yao-ch'en's poetry, though keeping step with Ou-yang Hsiu's, was consistently more delicate and more flavorful than that of his friend. He was in fact the finest poet of the first half of the eleventh century. In the grave inscription which Ou-yang Hsiu wrote for Mei, he mentions that as Mei's fame as a poet increased he was troubled by the number of people who came to him asking for poems. In spite of Ou-yang Hsiu's assertion, however, we do not find, among the 2800 poems that remain from Mei's hand, many that convey an impression of perfunctoriness.

In Ou-yang Hsiu's work entitled *Shih-hua,* or *Remarks on Poetry,* he records the following words of Mei Yao-ch'en which give some indication of the hard labor that lay behind his apparent calmness and ease: "Though the poet may put forth great effort, it is extremely difficult to choose words correctly. If he manages to use words with a fresh skill and to achieve some effect that no one before has ever achieved, then he may consider that he has done well. He must be able to paint some scene that is difficult to depict, in such a way that it seems to be right before the eyes of the reader and has an endless significance that exists outside the words themselves — only then can he be regarded as great" (35:128/5a).

Of Mei's character, Ou-yang Hsiu wrote that he was "lofty of will, pure in action, refined in manner, and mild in expression" (35:64/7b); and of his appearance, he said, "his dress and way of walking had the solemnity befitting a Confucian" (35:42/10b).

Su Shun-ch'in (1008–1048)

In addition to Mei Yao-ch'en, there was another poet who was much encouraged and patronized by Ou-yang Hsiu, though he never became the artistic equal of Ou-yang Hsiu, much less of Mei Yao-ch'en. His name was Su Shun-ch'in, and he was the son of a distinguished family, both his father and grandfather having held the post of prime minister. He himself held a position in the Chin-tsou-yüan, a department of the government whose function was to distribute edicts and forward memorials to the proper authorities, but he was impeached by a rival group in the administration on charges of having sold waste paper from the office trash baskets and used the money to call singing girls to the office, where he held a drinking party. He retired to Suchow far to the south in Kiangsu, where he bought a villa which he named Ts'ang-lang-t'ing, or Sea Blue Pavilion, and lived out the rest of his days, dying at the comparatively early age of forty-one. He is said to have been extremely interested in military matters, and seems to have been in all a rather rash man with a fondness for the gallant manner. In a seven-character regulated poem, "In Front of the Mirror," he has left us the following self-portrait.

Iron face, blue-grey beard, eyes with sharp points:
I must be a frightening sight to the boys and girls of the world.
In my heart I've vowed to my country to put down the barbarians at last,
But Fate gives me no chance – I must retire and take up farming.
A taste for letters, a fondness for brush and ink – not for me!
It makes me sigh – all these ills only advance my style.
All my life my energy burns bright as the Dipper stars –
Stupid bronze! Who can see anything clearly in you?   (42:7/6b)

The barbarians referred to are the two states which were troubling the peace of China at this time, Liao in the north and Hsi-hsia in the west. The "stupid bronze" is the mirror.

The following poem, called "Evening, Anchored at Tu-t'ou," is considered to be one of the finest poems in the seven-character *chüeh-chü* form dating from the Sung. It was probably written when the poet was on his way south from the capital to Suchow.

Spring haze lies on the fields, grass is doubly green;
At moments, unseen flowers come to light in a single tree.
By evening we anchor the lone boat at the foot of an old shrine;
As wind and rain fill the river, we watch the tide come in.

(42:7/3b)

Fan Chung-yen (989–1052), Han Ch'i (1008–1075), and Shao Yung (1011–1077)

Before concluding this chapter I should point out that the world of poetry in the first half of the eleventh century was not completely dominated by the men discussed above — Ou-yang Hsiu, Mei Yao-ch'en, and Su Shun-ch'in. The new ideal of the statesman who is at the same time a cultural leader of the nation is reflected not only in Ou-yang Hsiu, but in the other *Ming-ch'en,* or "famous statesmen," of the period who held important posts in the government. Such men as Fan Chung-yen, Fu Pi, Wen Yen-po, and Han Ch'i, while they wrote much prose dealing mainly with political problems, also wrote poetry. The eldest of the group, Fan Chung-yen (989–1052), is a good example. A statesman and general of great ability and fame, he displayed skill in the writing of poetry, as the following example will show, a five-character regulated poem named "The Color of the Fields." Here, to borrow Mei Yao-ch'en's words on the task of the poet quoted above, he has succeeded in painting a "scene that is difficult to depict, in such a way that it seems to be right before the eyes of the reader."

It is not smoke, nor is it mist,
Silently shining on top of the tower.
A white bird suddenly tears it apart
And the setting sun opens it up with light.
Would it come to an end with the fragrant grass?
Perhaps it has come chasing that distant sail.
Who understands the intention of Lord Shan,
Climbing high, getting drunk, and then going home?

(17:3/4b)

The last couplet is an allusion to the third-century general and statesman Shan Chien. He was assigned to guard the border of the empire against enemy invasion, and is said to have often held banquets and drinking parties out in the fields in order to instill in his troops a feeling of safety and security. Fan Chung-yen held a similar position, guarding China against the Hsi-hsia state, and as he drank with his staff on the top of a hill and looked down at the hazy fields of spring, he was conscious of the grave responsibilities of his post. Because Fan Chung-yen is of an older generation than Ou-yang Hsiu and Mei Yao-ch'en, we may still see in his work the influence of the rather precious Hsi-k'un style that dominated the poetry of the early Sung.

By contrast, the following poem by Han Ch'i (1008–1075), an elder associate of Ou-yang Hsiu and an important statesman in the late years of Emperor Jen-tsung's reign, is wholly in the new style of Sung poetry. Entitled "Suffering from the Heat," it is in five-character old-poetry form. The date indicated in the opening lines of the poem corresponds to July 17, 1051. Fu-sang, in line five, is a legendary tree that grows in the midst of the eastern sea and from which the sun rises; the Crow of the Yang [3] in line seven is the crow which, according to Chinese folklore, lives in the sun.

> Summer, the year *hsin-mao* of the *Huang-yu* era,
> First of the sixth month: the dog days.
> Seven days after their beginning,
> The heat has reached its fiercest peak.
> The glowing sun, having scorched Fu-sang,
> Blazes away in the direction of noon.
> The Crow of the Yang consumes himself with fire;
> His wings droop and do not bear him west.
> The waves of the four seas tremble with heat
> And all heaven and earth begin to simmer and stew.
> Dragons hide in their deepest caves,
> Sweating, gasping, not daring to make rain.
> The Thunder God clasps his drumsticks and flees,
> Heedless that the carriage shakes his drum to pieces.
> Haven't we the depths of our rooms and halls?
> The air in them is as close as though kettles were boiling,

[3] Yang: the positive principle of heat, light, masculinity, activity, as opposed to cold, darkness, femininity, passivity [Tr.].

Haven't we the heights of our terraces and towers?
The wind is as foul as though burdened with plague.
I almost wonder if all creatures on earth
Are about to be turned into smoke-cured meat.
Once I heard, between K'un and Lang
There's a separate world of gods and immortals,
Where *lei-san* washes the troubled heart
And jade nectar cleanses the tainted bowels.
How I wish that I could fly there –
But it wouldn't be right if I went alone!
And how could all the men in the world
All on the same day sprout such wings?   (1:5a)

The last section of the poem is a reference to the mythical lands of K'un-lun and Lang-feng, the home of the immortals. The meaning of the words *lei-san* is unknown. The ending of the poem recalls Tu Fu's wish, expressed in his "Song on How the Autumn Wind Blew the Thatch off My House," that he might somehow get a huge roof that would shelter all the poor people of the world, and may possibly be a conscious imitation of it. By 1051, when this poem was written, Han Ch'i was already a high official, and it is important to note that a man in his position should have had this sense of responsibility for the comfort and welfare of "all the men in the world."

The following poem, a seven-character *chüeh-chü* called "A Gathering of Eight Old Men," gives an interesting glimpse into the bureaucratic world of the time. It was written by an official named Han Wei (1017–1098), whose father and elder brother were also officials and who, on occasion, exchanged poems with Ou-yang Hsiu, Mei Yao-ch'en, Su Shun-ch'in, Ssu-ma Kuang, and Wang An-shih. The poem was written at a gathering of eight elderly officials, all of whom came from the same town, received their *chin-shih* degree the same year, and were attached to the same government office. The scene is strikingly similar to a gathering of prominent Japanese politicians and businessmen who were graduated from the same high school in prewar days and who have come together to eat, drink, sing old school songs, and reminisce. The main difference is that the leaders of Sung society were also able to write poetry — indeed were expected to be able to do so as one of their qualifications for leadership.

Took degrees the same year, same office, same town;
Hair peppered with grey or all white, we sit down to a splendid spread.
After three cups, ears burn, singing voices sound out.
How fine – to be as merry as in the days when we were young!

(34:32b)

By this time we no longer find many men who like Lin Pu in the earlier years of the Sung, wrote poetry but remained private citizens all their lives. The reason probably is that if a man had learning and ability enough to write poetry he could, through the examination system, enter the official world and secure a post in the government. If we were to look for examples of poetry written by private citizens of this period, we would find an interesting one in the *Chi-jang-chi*, a collection of peculiar poems by a peculiar man, the philosopher Shao Yung (1011–1077), whose name has already been mentioned in the Introduction. He lived all his life in semiseclusion in a house which he called An-lo-wo, or Comfortable Den, in Loyang. A poem entitled "Song of the Water Willow in Front of Comfortable Den" describes his home:

In front of Comfortable Den, by a little crooked stream,
New rushes, a delicate willow, turn green year by year.
Before my eyes a procession of good sights pass –
Who says that life is so full of wants?   (57:13/43b)

The following poem, in five-character lines, is called "Song of Delight."

Rejoice and rejoice again,
Be glad and be glad once more!
Fine fellows to become my friends,
Beautiful sights to fill my view,
Good wine to be my drink,
Good food to be my fare,
Born, grew up, and now I grow old
All in a time of perfect peace!   (57:10/146b)

All of Shao Yung's several hundred poems bear titles with the word *yin*, "Song of . . ." The following "Song of Severe Illness" is the last poem he wrote:

Born into a world of peace,
Brought up in a world of peace,
Grew old in a world of peace,
Going to die in a world of peace:
You ask how old I am?
Sixty-seven, that's my age.
I look up, I look down, between heaven and earth,
Exultant and free from all shame.   (57:19/136b)

To the eye of the professional poet, this may seem too blatant in its philosophy and too lacking in poetic refinement. But Sung poetry is forever reasoning with itself, and Shao Yung's poems may perhaps be best regarded as uninhibited extensions of this trait.

Loyang, the Western Capital, seems in Northern Sung times to have been a peaceful place to live, and Shao Yung was not the only distinguished man who savored its quiet and seclusion. The famous statesman and historian Ssu-ma Kuang (1019–1086), because of his opposition to the reforms of Wang An-shih, which will be described in the following chapter, retired from political life and took up residence in Loyang. It was there that he brought to completion his colossal history in 294 *chüan*, the *Tzu-chih t'ung-chien*, or *General Mirror for the Aid of Government*.

Chapter Four

LATE PERIOD OF THE

NORTHERN SUNG

1050–1100

Wang An-shih (1021–1086)

It was only natural that Ou-yang Hsiu, the leader of the poetic and cultural world of the first half of the eleventh century, should search for a successor to carry on the work of disseminating to the new generation the literary and philosophical innovations which he himself had made. In this task he put great hopes in two young men of talent, Wang An-shih and Su Tung-p'o. Both men in time became leaders and arbiters of the latter half of the eleventh century, in the realm of poetry and in the broader realm of the nation's political and cultural development. But the two men did not follow the same road. Though Su Tung-p'o worked faithfully to carry on the ideals of Ou-yang Hsiu, Wang An-shih found himself compelled to disagree with them. Both men, it may be noted, became finer poets than Ou-yang Hsiu — in particular Su Tung-p'o, who became the outstanding poet of the Northern Sung period — though Wang An-shih was a master in his own right.

Wang An-shih, because of the program of political and economic reforms which he instituted, has attracted the interest, and often the admiration, of historians in recent years. But older historians did not hold him in such high esteem. From the twelfth century, shortly after his death, until the beginning of the present century, he was more often regarded by Chinese historians as an extremist who attempted to push through reforms that were too radical and unpractical, and this view was accepted by the Confucian scholars of Japan as well.

Whatever his reputation as a statesman may have been in the past, however, his status as a major poet has, from Southern Sung times until the present, remained unquestioned. His complete works contain thirty-seven *chüan* of poetry, representing approximately 400 old poems and 1000 in regulated verse, or *chüeh-chü* form.

Wang An-shih was born in 1021, the year before Emperor Jentsung's accession to the throne. In 1042, at the age of twenty-two, he received his *chin-shih* degree, coming out fourth in a group of 839 candidates who took the examination that year. Ou-yang Hsiu, who by this time held an important position in the government, took careful note of this talented young man, who was fourteen years his junior and came from the same region in Kiangsi, and worked, with the cooperation of other high officials, to secure good posts for him in the central government. Wang An-shih himself maintained a rather cool attitude toward these men, however, and for the duration of Emperor Jentsung's reign, while Ou-yang Hsiu and his group held the place of power in the government, he actually requested to be assigned to posts in the provinces. He justified this unusual choice by saying that his pay went farther at such provincial posts, and that the work allowed him greater leisure for study. In a poem written at this period, he remarked:

> What would I know about governing the people?
> I want an out-of-the-way place where I can steal some time.
>
> (55:10/6a)

But it would seem that Wang An-shih had other reasons for requesting duty in the provinces. Ou-yang Hsiu and the men of his generation were proud of the way they had restored Confucianism to its former position of supremacy in the world of thought, and of the new cultural and spiritual order which they had brought to the nation. And yet the principles of the new order were not proving at all effective in practical application. During the periods that Confucian scholars looked upon as ideal — those of the sage rulers Yao and Shun and of the three ancient dynasties of Hsia, Shang, and Chou — the government had placed the welfare and happiness of the people above all other concerns. As Wang An-shih eyed his seniors in the government, however, he saw them making little effort to re-create this ideal in the present. And his suspicion and disgust were increased by what he saw of the hard life of the common people in his dealings with them as an official in the provinces.

In a five-character old poem written at this time he attacked the "land-grabbing" of the big landlords and praised the system of antiquity with its absence of private property:

The Three Dynasties of old looked after the peasants as their children;
There was no distinction between public and private wealth.

(55:6/4b)

In another poem of the same form, in which he urges that the government granaries be opened in order to relieve famine, he declared that

Later ages do not return to the old ways;
Land-grabbing – that's the cause of this poverty!

(55:17/4b)

and expressed his longing to rescue the people from hardship by returning to the practices of antiquity.

But there were few of his companions and associates who could understand his ambitions. In a seven-character regulated verse, addressed to his friend Wu Chi-yeh, he describes his feelings:

Chasing north and south, my clothes have been spoiled by wind and dust;
My will grows lax and careless – already I bring shame to my parents.
The common lot are still suspicious of my fastidious approach;
My friends scoff at my devotion to party affairs.
I think of the pleasure of joining the fish far away in the Hao;
I would startle the seagulls – an old man ashamed on the beach.
Now suddenly I've found you – but that it had to be so late!
How long it's been with no one who could understand my thoughts.

(55:31/1a)

The fifth line is an allusion to the story of how, in ancient times, the philosophers Chuang Tzu and Hui Tzu walked by the Hao River and debated the question of whether fish are really happy (*Chuang Tzu* sec. 17). The following line refers to a story in *Lieh Tzu*, sec. 2, of a child who was in the habit of playing on the seashore with the gulls;

one day he was asked by his father to catch one of the gulls, but when he went as usual to the shore, he found that none of the gulls would come near him. Wang An-shih is implying that his own actions in the same way startle and repel the men of the world.

The following poem, in five-character old form, was written around the same time and conveys the poet's feelings in symbolic terms.

> The sun is lusterless above the city;
> As autumn comes, its brilliance fades.
> A mass of cold air floods even the sky;
> What then of the humble grass and trees?
> Yellow chrysanthemums, perfect in nature,
> Lone flowers defying the press of the mob,
> Among the dew and frost, I pick and pick you.
> You will serve to still my morning hunger.
>
> (55:11/2a)

The first four lines probably refer to the nation which, although it seems to be enjoying an era of peace and prosperity, is actually entering upon a period of autumnal decline. The cold air is already upon the world, bringing suffering especially to the "grass and trees," probably a symbol of the common people. In the latter part of the poem, the yellow chrysanthemum "defying the press of the mob" is certainly meant to represent the poet himself. The eating of chrysanthemum petals is an allusion to the poet Ch'ü Yüan (ca. 300 B.C.), who in his long poem, the *Li sao,* or *Encountering Sorrow,* pictures himself eating this most refined of foods.

Wang An-shih did not spend all his time in provincial posts, but occasionally occupied positions in the capital as well. When he was in the capital, however, he did not usually attend the frequent banquets to which his fellow officials invited him, he tells us; nor would he serve wine when guests came to call on him, his only interest apparently being in his library:

> I hold a post at court, it's true,
> But seldom have occasion to drink;
> I pile up stacks of books on my wall,
> But put out no wine cup when guests drop in.
>
> (55:16/3b)

He also seems to have been negligent about paying social calls on his superiors:

> It's human nature to enjoy being fawned on;
> I alone seldom bother to pay calls.
> I'm on very poor terms with men of influence,
> And everything I do seems to go clumsily.

(55:11/4a)

Wang An-shih first met Ou-yang Hsiu in 1056, when, at thirty-six, he had been assigned to a post in the capital. Ou-yang Hsiu, obviously pleased at the meeting, declared in a poem written on the occasion, "Always I've regretted only hearing your name and never getting to know you," adding, "In the years to come, who will be able to compete with you?" (35:57/1a) — an indication that he would like Wang An-shih to be his successor. Wang An-shih displayed the respect demanded by courtesy, but seems to have taken a rather noncommittal attitude toward the elder statesman.

Wang An-shih's reputation as a man of extraordinary integrity continued to grow, along with rumors of his stubbornness and eccentricity. Various stories illustrating the latter qualities have been handed down, though it is quite possible that they are fabrications of Wang's political rivals. Among these is the story of how Wang, invited along with other officials to the customary "Party for Viewing Flowers and Catching Fish" held each spring at the imperial palace, ate up a whole golden plate full of fish food, apparently under the impression that it was intended for the guests. Emperor Jen-tsung, when told of the incident, remarked that if he had indeed made such a mistake, he might have stopped eating after the first mouthful, when he must surely have become aware of his mistake, but that to eat up the whole plateful was a mark of sheer obstinacy. Another story tells how Su Tung-p'o's father Su Hsün, having met Wang An-shih at Ou-yang Hsiu's house, was appalled by his untidy hair and dirty dress; in order to warn people against such a man, he composed his famous essay, *Pien-chien-lun*, or "Essay on Recognizing a Scoundrel," in which he declared that such a lack of attention to one's personal appearance indicated a dangerous absence of common sense and human feeling.

In a mood of irritability and isolation, Wang An-shih reached the age where he began to feel old. A poem in seven-character regulated verse, one of two written for his childhood friend Teng Tzu-i, describes his feelings:

> In Green Valley, when we first met, it was green spring for
>   us both;
> Old now and far away, I face the stream with flagging spirit.
> All things one by one follow the waves and go;
> Year by year I get more of these useless new grey hairs.
> To speak from the heart, I can't bear to abandon the "hori-
>   zontal eyed,"
> Though in dealing with the world, I fear I draw near the
>   "bristling scales."
> Words of praise – I thank you for the generous way you treat
>   me,
> And regret that my talents are no better than average.

(55:32/5a)

Green Valley is the name of a place in Nanking where Wang An-shih had spent his youth. In the second poem he recalls that when he and Teng Tzu-i were young, "We would gather handfuls of new rushes and plait them together." But now, as he faces the flowing waters of the stream, the symbol in Chinese literature of the passing of time, he realizes that he has reached the age when his energies are beginning to wane. The phrase "horizontal-eyed" in the fifth line is taken from *Chuang Tzu*, sec. 12, and refers to the common people, whom Wang An-shih longs to help. "Bristling scales," in the following line, refers to the deadly scales that bristle from the throat of the dragon, a metaphor for the anger of the ruler derived from *Han Fei Tzu*, sec. 12. Wang is probably referring in particular to the famous "Ten Thousand Word Memorial," a proposal for government reforms which he had submitted to Emperor Jen-tsung at this time, and which he feared might incur the emperor's wrath.

Wang An-shih's chance came at last when, after the tediously long reign of Emperor Jen-tsung, and that of his sickly successor, Emperor Ying-tsung, a new ruler came to the throne in 1068. Known as Emperor Shen-tsung, he was only twenty when he became ruler. Wang An-shih, forty-nine, at the time, was chosen to fill the highest post in the government and, as is well known, set about to fulfill the ambitions he had nursed for so long by instituting his so-called "New Laws," a reform program that centered upon the strengthening of national defense and the improvement of the lot of the farmers. Ou-yang Hsiu, Han Ch'i, Fu Pi, and the other elder statesmen of the time, men who in the past had been enthusiastic supporters of Wang, looked on with disapproval. The disapproval of his seniors was in time matched by that of many of his contemporaries and successors, and he left behind him when he died a bad reputation that continued unchallenged until the present century, when historians with new viewpoints and new interests have in some cases completely reversed the judgment of the past. Whether he cared what it might do to his reputation or not, Wang An-shih seems not to have hesitated to criticize his seniors in government. It is even said that on one occasion he advised Emperor Jen-tsung that Ou-yang Hsiu was the kind of man who, "if he were in office in a district, would ruin the district, and if in office in the imperial court, would ruin the court" (54:17, under "Hsi-ning 4th year").

Wang's hostility to his predecessors was not confined to the field of politics, but extended to that of literature as well. He agreed with Ou-yang Hsiu in his contempt for the Hsi-k'un style, which had dominated the poetry of the previous period, a point of view he expressed at an early stage in his "Preface to the Poems of Chang of the Bureau of Punishments" (31:84/9a). He also agreed with Ou-yang Hsiu in approving poetry that had some thought content, as evidenced by the examples of poems of political criticism which I have mentioned above, or by his poems modeled on the works of the T'ang Buddhist recluses Han-shan and Shih-te. All of these works, with their expressions of philosophy and political theory, may be regarded as extending and enlarging a direction that was first explored by Ou-yang Hsiu.

At the same time, however, Wang An-shih seems to have felt there was a danger that the kind of descriptive and philosophical poems which Ou-yang Hsiu had written and preferred might in time prove inimical to the lyricism that ought properly to underlie all poetic literature. On this point, as well as on points of political theory, he found himself in opposition to Ou-yang Hsiu.

We may note first of all that he was very critical of Han Yü, the poet of the past whom Ou-yang Hsiu had praised so highly. His criticisms are expressed in the following seven-character *chüeh-chü.* While belittling Han Yü's contribution to the advancement of poetry, he perhaps is also expressing an indirect criticism of Ou-yang Hsiu.

In the muddle they slip away – the hundred years of life,
And in all the world, how many men know the Way that's true?
He worked to get rid of worn-out diction, putting on a show for the crowd.
Too bad he wore out his energies contributing nothing!   (55:48/6b)

If Wang An-shih thought little of Han Yü, there was one poet of the T'ang whom he admired intensely — Tu Fu. As I have noted earlier, Tu Fu's standing in Chinese literature was not fixed before the time of Wang An-shih. Ou-yang Hsiu found certain aspects of Tu Fu's poetry displeasing, but Wang An-shih's admiration and respect for him were unqualified. In a poem in old form entitled "Portrait of Tu Fu," he writes:

> When I read the poems of Shao-ling [Tu Fu],
> I think I'm in the presence of the primal spirit!

And he concludes by saying:

> If only you could rise from the dead
> And come here to be my companion!
>
>   (55:13/1a)

The view commonly accepted today that Tu Fu surpassed all other poets of past and present was first expressed by Wang An-shih.

Tu Fu's influence is clearly to be seen in Wang An-shih's regulated verse pieces such as the five-character poem called "Travel Thoughts," probably written during the period when Wang had not yet won favor:

> Going north and south, this body grows old;
> Anxious, I ask about the road.
> Earth is broad – it holds the three lands of Ch'u;
> Sky is low – it dips into the five lakes.
> Watching clouds, my mind goes with them far away;
> Walking in the moon, my shadow, like it, is alone.

My melancholy rises with the autumn wind
But my sad song is not for the perch of home.

(55:23/3a)

The last line is an allusion to the story of Chang Han of the Chin dynasty who, when autumn wind arose, recalled the fresh perch, vegetables, and other good things of his native region of Wu. (See his biography in *Chin shu, chüan* 92.) T'ang Keng, a scholar writing at the end of the Northern Sung, pointed out that the third and fourth lines are "a type of construction taken from Tzu-mei [Tu Fu]" (55: 23/3a, quoted in Li Pi's commentary). He might have gone on to note that the two lines which follow are also modeled on lines by Tu Fu in his poem entitled "The Yangtze and the Han," which read:

A scrap of cloud, like myself, far off in the sky;
Through the long night, the moon, like me, alone.

(14:2523)

As one might expect, the quality which Wang An-shih most admired in Tu Fu was his love and concern for the common people. But he also admired, I believe, the lyricism that went with Tu Fu's social consciousness. He disagreed with Ou-yang Hsiu on the relative merits of Tu Fu and Li Po. As I have mentioned earlier, Ou-yang Hsiu admired Li Po for his freedom of spirit and placed him above Tu Fu. Wang An-shih, when he compiled his *Ssu-chia shih-hsüan*, or *Selections from Four Poets*, an anthology of the poems of Tu Fu, Ou-yang Hsiu, Han Yü, and Li Po, arranged the poets in that order. According to a work called the *Chung-shan yü-lu* (now lost but quoted in a collection of critical remarks, the *T'iao-ch'i yü-yin ts'ung-hua*), Wang An-shih explained why he placed Li Po last by saying that Li Po's poems were "mean and low in outlook" and that "of ten poems, nine are about women or wine" (47: Part I, 6/4b). If Wang An-shih really dismissed Li Po's poetry so summarily, his view was certainly a shallow one. The Southern Sung poet Lu Yu, in his collection of writings, the *Lao-hsüeh-an pi-chi*, remarks, "I suspect that Wang An-shih did not really say this" (29:6/57).

Wang An-shih seems to have been anxious not only to establish the worth of Tu Fu alone, but to reappraise the whole lyric spirit of T'ang poetry. He compiled an anthology of T'ang poetry entitled *T'ang pai-chia shih-hsüan*, or *Selections from One Hundred T'ang Poets*, selecting poems from the collected works of over a hundred poets which his friend Sung Min-ch'iu had lent him. Though one may not always concur with his choice of poems, his work is important for being one of the earliest anthologies of T'ang poetry made after the close of the T'ang. His "hundred poets" include men such as Hsü Hun, Han Wo, and other late T'ang poets noted for their sentimental style. It is said that Wang An-shih, in his late years, reappraised the work of Li Shang-yin, the late T'ang poet whose works had been so assiduously imitated by the Hsi-k'un style poets of the early Sung. He expressed the opinion that no other poet in the T'ang had so skillfully imitated the style of Tu Fu, pointing as an example to such lines of Li Shang-yin as the following:

> The dimly shining lake does not receive the moon;
> The evening breeze is about to sink into the hills.
>
> (14:6223)

His views are to be found in *chüan* 22 of the *T'iao-ch'i yü-yin ts'ung-hua*, which quotes them from the now lost *Ts'ai K'uan-fu shih-hua*.

It would seem an anomaly that a great political leader like Wang An-shih should have had such a fondness for poetry that was purely lyrical, and consequently extremely apolitical in nature. But both tastes probably sprang from the same quality which stood at the very center of his personality — his fastidiousness. He seems to have felt strongly that lyricism should always be regarded as the essence of poetry. Certainly there is a higher proportion of lyricism in his own verse than is to be found in that of his contemporaries.

During the time when he held office as prime minister — a period which lasted until 1076 — he wrote relatively few poems, as might be expected. When the success of his reform program appeared to be certain, he turned over the leadership of political affairs to his associate Lü Hui-ch'ing and others of his group, and retired to Chiang-ning, the present-day city of Nanking. He was nominally a native of Kiangsi Province, though in fact his real home was Nanking.

In a poem of seven-character regulated verse, "Written after the Rain Passed," we find the following lines which describe in symbolic terms the poet's retirement:

> Who like the floating cloud knows how to advance and retire?
> After bringing a spell of rain, it returns to the hills.
>
> (55:31/4b)

Wang An-shih lived in a small country house that was situated seven li from the eastern gate of the city of Nanking and seven li from Mount Chiang, one of the famous spots in the eastern suburbs. Because of its location, he gave his house the name Pan-shan, or "Halfway to the Mountain." There was no wall around the house, and when someone advised him to build one, it is said that he merely laughed and gave no answer. He spent his days visiting temples in the neighborhood, riding a donkey and accompanied by several servants. He disliked riding in a palanquin because he considered it an inhuman way to travel.

Thus, during the last years of Emperor Shen-tsung's reign, Wang spent his time in retirement, reading, meditating, writing, and composing poetry. Many of his poems of this period, particularly those in the seven-character *chüeh-chü* form, describe the scenery around him. In a poem written in his youth he had stated:

> It is rather among the hills and streams
> That my desires are most often fulfilled;
>
> (55:10/4a)

and he continued in his later years to show a great fondness for nature. I shall quote a few examples of his poems written during the period of retirement, all of them in seven-character *chüeh-chü* form. In the first of these the poet seems, in spite of his distaste for palanquins, to have traveled by one on this particular outing, or at least to have asked to have one follow him for the journey home.

> Who brings stove blacking to dye the spring tide dark?
> Who twists yellow gold to fashion willow limbs?
> The west hills, the east moat, from now on will be good.
> Follow me with the bamboo chair – don't balk because it's far!
>
> (55:41/5b)

Willows, apricot blossoms – what place is best?
From stone bridges and rush roofs, rain has dried at last.
Green hangs over the quiet road, inviting a rest in deep shade;
Pink falls on the clear pond, where happily I get a closer look.

(55:42/8a)

And in the midst of the purity and cleanness of nature, the life of the peasants, for whose welfare Wang An-shih had taken such thought, unfolded before his eyes. In the following poem called "Ch'ing-ming," or "Spring Festival," he gives us a glimpse of that life. There has been a celebration in the village, and now the crowds are breaking up. Some men lie asleep in the grass, empty bottles beside them, while beyond the embankment a party is still going on.

In the town to the east, drinkers scatter, evening sun is slow;
By the road to the south, children's swings dangle silent and still.
Men with tall bottles lie in the fragrant grass;
Wind bringing shrill flutes comes from the green embankment.

(55:41/2b)

The last eight years of Emperor Shen-tsung's reign were named the era of *Yüan-feng*, or "Wealth of the People." The following poem, the first of a group entitled "Songs of *Yüan-feng*," describes the bountiful harvest that was reaped in the fall of the first year of the new era, 1078.

Water fills the dammed-up pond, grain fills the basket.
Wildly they cart off fruit and vegetables but still there's more to be picked.
Here and there from the sacred grove comes the sound of pipe and drum;
Together we make offerings this first fall of *Yüan-feng*.   (55:41/1a)

Wang An-shih's last years were ones of disappointment. In 1085 Emperor Shen-tsung died, and the New Laws party fell from power. It was replaced by a conservative group headed by Ssu-ma Kuang, who set about putting an end, one by one, to the reforms which Wang and his group had instituted. Wang died in the fourth month of the following year, 1086.

Wang An-shih's poetry, like his personality and his politics, is marked by fastidiousness and sensitivity, its lyricism deriving from the latter quality. In refusing to become preoccupied with sorrow, he resembles the other poets of the Sung, though in his case it was probably his discrimination as a scholar and a statesman which led him to put a restraint on sadness. In a seven-character regulated verse written to comfort a certain Li Chang, probably a younger friend of the poet who had failed to pass the civil service examination, he states the opinion that "Writing should particularly avoid too frequent sorrow" (55: 34/2a).

I shall close with two more examples of poems by Wang An-shih in five-character *chüeh-chü* form. The first is entitled "Fragrant Grass," the second "Plum Flowers." They may be read as self-portraits of the sensitive and fastidious poet himself.

> Fragrant grass, who knows who planted you,
> Already spread in several clumps there by the terrace?
> You have no mind to compete with the world –
> What need is there for this deep rich green?   (55:40/9a)

> At the corner of the wall, a few branches of plum
> Brave the cold to blossom alone.
> Even far off, I know it isn't snow
> Because of the hidden fragrance that comes.   (55:40/10b)

Su Tung-p'o

The greatest of the Sung poets was Su Shih, better known by his literary name Su Tung-p'o (1037–1101). His father, Su Hsün, and his younger brother, Su Ch'e, were also men of letters, and all three are numbered among the "Eight Prose Masters of the T'ang and Sung." As a poet, however, Su Tung-p'o stands far above his father and brother.

Su Tung-p'o was born fifteen years after Wang An-shih, the man who was to become his political rival. He received his *chin-shih* degree fifteen years after Wang, and he died fifteen years after him — a series of coincidences that can only be called uncanny. He was born in the district of Mei-shan in Szechwan on the nineteenth day of the twelfth lunar month of the third year of the *Ching-yu* era, a date which would fall in the early days of 1037. He and his younger brother Su Ch'e received their *chin-shih* degrees in 1057, the thirty-sixth year of Emperor Jen-tsung's reign. The head of the examining committee on that occasion was Ou-yang Hsiu, and Mei Yao-ch'en was one of the committee members. In traditional China, where formal schooling tended to be nominal and real learning was done at home under hired tutors, the relationship between teacher and disciple was less important than that between the students who took the civil service examination and the head of the examining committee, for those who passed the examination looked upon the head of the examining committee as their true teacher. Su Tung-p'o and his brother thus became disciples of Ou-yang Hsiu and entered the political and literary world as such. It would appear that Ou-yang Hsiu, who at first had placed high hopes in Wang An-shih, was by this time becoming fully aware of Wang's opposition to him, and he therefore transferred his expectations to his new disciple, the brilliant Su Tung-p'o. He is said to have remarked of Su Tung-p'o, "I am going to see to it that this man has room to grow in."

On the death of his mother, Su Tung-p'o, his father, and his brother all left the capital and returned to their home in Szechwan to observe the customary mourning period. In 1059 they set out for the capital again, sailing down the Yangtze in a boat. The following poem in seven-character old poetry form — "On the Yangtze Watching the Hills" — was written at this time as the party was passing through the San-hsia, or Three Gorges, section of the river. It is among the earliest of his extant poems.

> From the boat watching hills – swift horses;
> A hundred herds race by in a flash.
> Ragged peaks before us suddenly change shape,
> Ranges behind us start and rush away.
> I look up: a narrow trail angles back and forth,
> A man walking it, high in the distance.
> I wave from the deck, trying to call,
> But the lone sail takes us south like a soaring bird.*
>
> (43:1/10a)

The opening lines, in which the hills, as seen from the swiftly moving boat, are compared to herds of horses, display the acute observation, imagination, and skill in the use of metaphor that are to become the mark of his mature poetry; and the poet's efforts to call to the man in the distance are symbolic of the deep-felt love for his fellow men that underlies all his writing.

In 1061, at the age of twenty-six, the poet's official career began when he was appointed to a post in the district of Feng-hsiang in Shensi. When he was about thirty he returned to the capital and took up a post in the central government. One of his duties at this time was to receive the envoy from China's menacing neighbor to the north, the state of Liao. He himself tells us that the envoy memorized some of his writings, along with those of his father and brother. Already his fame as a man of letters was beginning to spread even beyond the borders of China.

When Ou-yang Hsiu died in 1072, Su Tung-p'o occupied the post of vice-governor of Hangchow in Chekiang. In the volume and reputation of his works he had already surpassed Ou-yang Hsiu as a literary figure, and his affable personality had attracted many men of ability to his side. In his career as an official, however, he did not advance smoothly. It was just at this time that Wang An-shih was beginning to put his New Laws into effect, and Su Tung-p'o, with his taste for freedom, seems to have had an instinctive dislike for them. His remark, made in a poem written for his brother Su Ch'e, or Tzu-yu, called "Joking with Tzu-yu," that "I will read ten thousand books but spare me the ones on law!" (43:7/13a) is famous. Wang An-shih's reforms seemed to him to be an attempt at control through inflexible laws, and he disliked and criticized them as a burden to the people. Among the reforms which Su Tung-p'o opposed most violently were those made in the examination system, by which Wang An-shih put greater emphasis upon the divisions known as *ching-i* or "explication of the Classics," and *lun-ts'e*, or "discussion of politics," and abolished the division on poetry, which up until this time had been the heart of the examination. It was probably because of his opposition on this score that Su was transferred from the post he had held in the capital to that of vice-governor of Hangchow. Wang An-shih, however, was a great enough man himself to recognize greatness in others. He gave warm praise to a poem which Su wrote in 1074 when serving as governor of Mi-chou in Shantung entitled "After Snow: Inscribed on North Terrace"; and, as already noted in the Introduction, his admiration led him to adopt the same set of rhymes in his own poems, composing six poems on Su's rhymes. Su's poem, one of two written on the same occasion in seven-character regulated verse, reads as follows:

> At twilight, fine rain was still falling,
> The night hushed and windless, the cold getting worse.
> Bedclothes felt as though they'd been drenched;
> I didn't know the courtyard was piled with drifts.
> Fifth watch: dawn light colors the study curtains;
> Under a half-moon, the cold rustle of painted eaves.
> I'll sweep North Terrace, have a look at Horse Ears Hill,
> Two peaks not yet shrouded in snow.*   (43:12/17b)

From the time when Wang An-shih turned the conduct of political affairs over to his associate Lü Hui-ch'ing and retired to the country, the atmosphere grew more sinister. In 1079, when Su Tung-p'o was serving as governor of Hu-chou in Chekiang, he was arrested, escorted to the capital, and confined in the Imperial Censorate prison. He was charged with "slandering the emperor" — that is, criticizing the government, and the evidence brought against him included lines in his poems such as that quoted above, "I will read ten thousand books but spare me the ones on law!" At the age of forty-four he prepared himself for death.

Because of extenuating circumstances, however, he was let off with a fairly light penalty — exile to the town of Huang-chou on the banks of the Yangtze in Hupei. Part of the period of exile he spent farming a plot of ground at a place called Tung-p'o, or Eastern Slope, from which he took his literary name. The poem called "Rain at the Time of Cold Food," already quoted in the Introduction, the two famous *fu*, or prose-poems, on the Red Cliff, and many other fine works date from the five years of his exile in Huang-chou. As a man who embraced a philosophy of resistance, as we shall see later, he was strong in the face of adversity, and exile gave him the opportunity to devote his energies with greater freedom than before to the interests of philosophy and literature.

In 1084, when Su was forty-nine, the restrictions upon his movement were eased and he traveled to Nanking to visit Wang An-shih, who was living there in retirement. The respect which the two men held for each other is revealed in the poems they composed on the occasion. Wang expressed great admiration for the lines in Su's poem written at that time which read:

The peaks are so crowded they neatly block the sun;
The river flows so far away it seems to bear up the sky . . .

(43:24/5a)

and composed a poem using the same rhymes. He showed his admiration for Su's personality when he remarked: "I do not know how many years it will be before another man like this appears!" In spite of their political differences, it would be a mistake to imagine the two men as narrowly partisan in their outlook.

The following year, when Emperor Jen-tsung died and his son Emperor Che-tsung came to the throne, with the new ruler's grandmother, the Empress Dowager, acting as regent, the political situation changed abruptly. The New Laws party fell from power and was replaced by the conservative group, the Old Laws party, with its leader, Ssu-ma Kuang, appointed as prime minister. The following year, 1086, saw the death of Wang An-shih, who had unhappily lived to witness the undoing of his reforms; Ssu-ma Kuang died shortly after. Su Tung-p'o took the latter's place as leader of the Old Laws party and, along with his brother Su Ch'e, became one of the most trusted ministers of the Empress Dowager. In the political world, Su Tung-p'o was looked upon as the heir of Ou-yang Hsiu. But he did not like to remain indefinitely in the capital, and again set out for the provinces, holding in succession the post of governor of Hangchow in Chekiang, of Ying-chou in Anhwei, and of Yang-chou in Kiangsu. "Where will I ever end my life?" he wrote. "My carriage wheels have rolled over half the world."

But with the death of the Empress Dowager in 1094, the political situation, like Su's carriage wheels, took another turn. The New Laws party came back to power and a new era name was proclaimed — Shao-sheng, or "Carrying on from the Sage" — a clear indication that Emperor Che-tsung from this time on intended to carry on the policies of his father, Emperor Shen-tsung. Su Tung-p'o was once more sent into exile, at first to the region of Hui-chou in Kwangtung, then to the farthest outpost of the empire, the island of Hainan in the South China Sea. Adversity once more helped to perfect his art, the result being the masterpieces which he wrote in Hainan known as "Tung-p'o's Overseas Writings."

When Emperor Che-tsung died in 1100 and his younger brother Emperor Hui-tsung came to the throne, things improved for Su Tung-p'o. A new era name was adopted, *Chien-chung-ching-kuo,* or "Rule of the Nation Based on the Mean," which indicated that the new regime was to strike a mean between the New Laws and Old Laws parties. Su Tung-p'o was allowed to leave his place of exile and was on his way north when he died at Ch'ang-chou in Kiangsu. It was the summer of 1101 and Su was sixty-six, the same age as Wang An-shih when he died.

It was not only in political matters that Wang An-shih and Su Tung-p'o differed. In personality they were opposites. The core of Wang An-shih's character was his fastidiousness, which found expression in his politics, his writings, and his daily life, and which people who did not understand him mistook at times for irascibility. By contrast, Su Tung-p'o was endowed with an innate freedom of spirit, and he gave the freest possible expression to his wide range of talents. As already noted, he was a master prose stylist and has left us the following description of his writing. "My writings are like the waters of an inexhaustible spring which spread out everywhere over the land. Along the level ground they surge and billow, flowing with ease a thousand li in a single day. And when they encounter hills and boulders, bends and turns, they take form from the things about them, though I do not know how they do it. All I know is that they always go where they should go, and stop where they should stop, that is all. Beyond that, even I do not understand" (52:1/30a).

He was also a noted calligrapher and painter, being one of the first of the so-called literary painters. He was skilled in conversation and loved a joke, qualities which especially endeared him to others. Though he liked many different kinds of men, and was liked in turn, it should not be thought that he was without convictions of his own. His philosophy is clearly stated in his poetry, as I shall demonstrate a little later. He was broad-minded and at the same time sensitive to details. An admirer of moderation, he was fond of wine but does not seem to have been able to drink very much. "I'm the kind of person who doesn't know how to drink, but only how to get drunk" (43:33/15a) he remarks of himself; and elsewhere he says, "I am a man who has always feared wine" (43:34/9a).

Su Tung-p'o's poetic works, in which he gives free and unrestrained expression to his rich and varied talent, are unmatched in stature by anything else in Sung poetry. First of all, he took over the interest in description that was already evident in the work of Ou-yang Hsiu and developed it to the fullest extent. As descriptions of objects we may note the series of poems written early in his career which he called "Eight Sights of Feng-hsiang," particularly that entitled "Song of the Stone Drums," while as descriptions of journeys or outings we should note his "Visit to Gold Mountain Temple" and "Hundred Pace Rapids," both of them remarkable for their keenness of observation, imaginativeness and use of simile. Because both these are rather lengthy, I shall quote a poem written early in 1077 when the poet was on his way from Mi-chou in Shantung to the capital. It is in five-character old form and bears this heading: "I was detained by a heavy snow at Wei-chou on New Year's Eve, but on the morning of the first day it cleared and I resumed my journey. Along the way, it started to snow again."

> New Year's Eve blizzard kept me from leaving;
> On the first, clear skies see me off.
> The east wind blows away last night's drunk;
> On a lean horse, I nod in the remains of a dream.
> Dim and hazy, the dawn light breaks through;
> Fluttering and turning, the last flakes fall.
> I dismount and pour myself a drink in the field –
> Delicious – but who to share it with?
> All at once evening clouds close down,
> Tumbling flurries that show no break.
> Flakes big as goose feathers hang from the horse's mane
> Till I think I'm riding a great white bird.
> Three years' drought plagues the east;
> Roofs sag on house rows, their owners fled.
> The old farmer lays aside his plow and sighs,
> Gulps tears that burn his starving guts.
> Spring snow falls late this year

> But spring wheat can still be planted.
> Do I grumble at the trials of official travel?
> To help you I'll sing a song of good harvest.*   (43:15/1a)

In his later years, Su's use of simile became freer than ever. When he was exiled to Hainan he described the journey which he made in a semicircle along the coast of the island, from Ch'iung-chou on the north shore to Tan-chou on the east shore as being "like following the rim of the crescent moon" (43:41/3b). Or, to turn to an example of simile applied to an intimate scene of daily life, he writes of his son thumping out the rhythm of the poems he has memorized:

> The little boy sits with book closed,
> Reciting poems from memory as though striking a lute.
>
> (43:42/4a)

But we should not let ourselves become too engrossed in the surface brilliance of Su's poetry; beneath this surface lies a deep and penetrating warmth of personality. Of the various tasks which the poet was able to accomplish, the most important was that of freeing Chinese poetry from the preoccupation with sorrow that had characterized it for so long.

I have already discussed in the Introduction this concern of earlier poetry with the theme of sorrow and have pointed out that one of the important accomplishments of Sung poetry was to escape from that preoccupation. The escape first became a real possibility with the poetry of Su Tung-p'o. Ou-yang Hsiu, before him, had moved in the direction of escape, though Ou-yang Hsiu himself was not fully conscious of that fact, and his method of escape was a negative one, seeking only to maintain a state of mental serenity.

In Su Tung-p'o's case, however, the escape was conscious and deliberate. He set about to transcend sorrow by means of a philosophy that viewed the infinite variety of human life with a largeness of vision that was equally varied. Moreover, he was able, because of the breadth and warmth of his personality, to expound his philosophy effectively in words. In the pages that follow I would like to trace in some detail in his poetry the logical development by which this broad-visioned philosophy took shape.

This new, broad-visioned philosophy of Su Tung-p'o is based upon the recognition that man's life does not consist of sorrow alone. Sorrow, to be sure, is to be found everywhere in life, and yet it is not the only element of which life is made. If there is sorrow, there is joy as well, the two intertwined like the strands of a rope. It is therefore foolish to become engrossed in the sorrowful side of life alone. Indeed, one should go a step further and examine whether those things which by ordinary standards are regarded as sorrows and misfortunes are really so or not. Looked at from the broader point of view, they may not be sorrows at all.

The following poem in five-character old form is an expression of this outlook. It was written shortly after the poet arrived in Huang-chou, his place of exile, and had moved from the quarters first assigned him to a slightly better house, the official lodge attached to the post station at a place called Lin-kao overlooking the Yangtze. The poem is called "Moving to Lin-kao Pavilion."

> Between heaven and earth I live,
> One ant on a giant grindstone,
> Trying in my petty way to walk to the right
> While the turning of the mill wheel takes me endlessly left.
> Though I go the way of benevolence and duty,
> I can't escape from hunger and cold.
> The sword-cooker – a perilous way to fix rice!
> The mat of spikes – no restful sitting there!
> But don't I have the beautiful hills and rivers?
> I no sooner turn my eyes than wind and rain bear them off.
> A man doesn't have to be old to retire,
> But how many have the daring to do it?
> Fortunately I've been turned out and abandoned,
> A weary horse with pack and saddle removed.
> All my family here, we have the run of the river post house.
> When things looked blackest, Heaven poked a hole for me.
> Hunger and poverty now multiplied, now divided,
> I don't see that I deserve either condolence or congratulation.
> Peaceful and calm, I have no joy or sorrow;
> My complaint has no reason to end with a *so!*   (43:20/24b)

The term in line four translated as "mill wheel," literally, "wind wheel," derives from Buddhist literature and refers to the forces which move the world. In lines seven and eight, the poet refers to two types of side-show performers, the man who prepares rice for cooking while seated on the point of a sword, and the man who sits down on a mat of spikes, suggesting that his own position may be equally perilous and uncomfortable. After referring to the beauties of the natural world and the fickleness with which they may be snatched from man's sight by storm and change, the poem takes a brighter turn. From the ordinary point of view, exile can only be considered a misfortune. And yet the poet, because he looks at life with a broader and more varied view, can speak of his exile as a fortunate occurrence. Perhaps his present situation is actually one of happiness, or at least will be the source from which some future happiness will spring. Or perhaps one should forget both sorrow and happiness and be content with a state of calm. The songs of the state of Ch'u in ancient times, most of them laments or complaints, employed an exclamatory particle pronounced *so* at the end of the lines to give the rhythm a rapid and forceful beat. But the poet in his new-won state of peace and calm has no need for such exclamations in his song.

Such is the general meaning of the poem. The line "Hunger and poverty now multiplied, now divided," reflects a philosophy of cyclical change such as is expressed in the *Book of Changes*. The outlook which regards misfortune as fortune, or which transcends such relative distinctions and value judgments, is based upon the philosophy of Chuang Tzu, particularly as it is expressed in the second chapter of the work which bears his name, the *Ch'i-wu-lun*, or "Discussion on Making All Things Equal."

Chuang Tzu's doctrine of "making all things equal" is only briefly touched upon in the poem quoted above. In the poem which I shall quote next, it appears much more clearly. This poem was written in 1071, when the poet, aged thirty-six, was on his way from the capital to Hangchow to assume the post of vice-governor. As he traveled down the Grand Canal, he stopped at Ch'en-chou in Honan to visit his younger brother Su Tzu-yu, who had, like the poet himself, clashed with Wang An-shih and had been assigned to an insignificant post in Ch'en-chou, referred to in the poem as Wan-ch'iu. After they had visited for some time, Su Tzu-yu accompanied his brother as far as Ying-chou in An-hwei, where they parted. The poem, in five-character old-form, is the second of two entitled "On Taking Leave of Tzu-yu at Ying-chou: Two Poems." The first, which begins

> The traveler's sails are spread in the west wind,
> Tears of parting fall into the clear Ying . . .

is given up to a mood of sorrow. But the second poem introduces the philosophy of the "equalization of things" as a means of transcending sorrow.

> Let the place be close by and parting faces hardly change;
> Let it be distant and tears wet our robes.
> But a foot apart, if we cannot meet,
> We might as well be parted a thousand miles.
> And if in life there were no partings,
> Who would know the gravity of love?
> When I first came to Wan-ch'iu
> The children danced and hung on my clothes.
> You knew then this sorrow was coming
> And begged me to stay till autumn winds pass.
> By now autumn winds are gone,
> But the sorrow of parting never ends.
> You ask when I'll be coming back?
> I answer, when the Year Star is in the east.
> Since parting and meeting are an endless cycle,
> Grief and joy must jostle each other.
> As we talk about it, we give great sighs –
> Our lives are like wind-blown tumbleweed.
> But too much worry brings the grey hairs early.
> Haven't you seen what it did to Master Six-one?

(43:6/21b)

The poem begins at once with a breadth of vision that transcends the distinctions of ordinary life. People are sorrowful when someone they love is going far away, but hardly disturbed at all if the destination is close by, though the fact of separation is exactly the same in both cases. To be consistent, therefore, we must either regard all partings as sorrowful, or admit that none of them really deserves to be lamented. Already the poet is seeking a broader view that will transcend sorrow. The couplet that follows is even more daring:

> And if in life there were no partings,
> Who could know the gravity of love?

Parting contains not only the negative element of sorrow, but a positive element as well; it serves to make us aware of the value of love. In this sense, should it not also be regarded as an occasion for happiness, or at least as a necessary step in the direction of future happiness? So far as I know, this view of the value of separation is original with Su Tung-p'o. I can recall nothing to match it in Chinese literature before him.

The breadth of vision with which the poem begins is not necessarily sustained throughout. In the central section the sadness of parting from his brother momentarily overwhelms the poet. The "Year Star" in line fourteen is the planet Jupiter, whose twelve-year cycle was used by the Chinese in measuring time. At the time when the poet was writing, Jupiter was in the northeast sector of the sky marked by the cyclical sign *hai*. Three years later, it would be dead east in the sector marked by the sign *yu*, and his term as vice-governor of Hangchow would be ended.

In the closing lines, the poet once more makes an effort to rise above his sorrow, this time by reference to the philosophy of cyclical change. His grief was in fact too strong in this case to be banished by the thought of future meetings and happiness, and led him to the simile of the wind-blown tumbleweed, which I shall have occasion to discuss later. But there is a final rallying of spirit in the last couplet, and the poem ends on a relatively light note with a reference to "Master Six-one," one of the names of Ou-yang Hsiu. Ou-yang Hsiu, the teacher of Su Tung-p'o and his brother, had retired this same year and was living in Ying-chou. Su Tung-p'o had of course gone to call on him and pay his respects when he passed through Ying-chou. It was the last meeting between teacher and disciple; Ou-yang Hsiu died the following year.

Though the poet makes the bold assertion that it is separation alone that teaches us the real value of love, he is not wholly successful in driving away sorrow. It would almost appear, in fact, that his efforts to do so on occasion only lead him deeper into grief. And yet the underlying tenor of the poem is one of transcendence of sorrow through greater breadth of vision.

This, then, is the first stage of Su Tung-p'o's philosophy. As we have seen, the doctrines upon which it is based are not original with him, but derive partly from the *Chuang Tzu* and partly from the view of cyclical change expressed in the *Book of Changes.* What is new and original with Su, I believe, is the attitude which recognizes sorrow as a necessary and inescapable element of life, but considers an exclusive preoccupation with sorrow to be ridiculous.

It was always easy for Confucianism, with its strong element of idealism, to visualize a society without sorrow. The sadness and indignation expressed by the poets in the *Book of Odes* are the sadness and indignation of men who had hoped for better things, but whose hopes have been betrayed, and the same, I believe, may be said of the poetry of Tu Fu in the T'ang period. This was not true of Su Tung-p'o who asserted that sorrow, and the misfortunes that are the cause of sorrow, are omnipresent in human life and constitute one of its inescapable elements. As long as the possibility of conflict exists between the individual and society, or between desire and fate, he perceived that sorrow would always be a necessary part of human life.

As an illustration of Su's view of the omnipresence of sorrow, we may look at a poem written in 1079, eight years after the one quoted above, when the poet was transferred from the post of governor of Hsü-chou in Kiangsu to that of governor of Hu-chou in Chekiang. He had been a good governor, and when he prepared to leave Hsü-chou, the people flocked to see him off and even tried to prevent his departure. The poem, in five-character old form, is the first of five written at the time to be sent to his brother and bearing the title, "I have left my post in Hsü-chou and am proceeding to Nan-ching; I am writing these on horseback to send to Tzu-yu."

> Clerks, townsmen, don't hang on me!
> Songs, flutes, don't sob like that!
> My life is made of sojourns only;

Is this the first time I've had to take leave?
Separation follows us everywhere;
Sadness and fret are bound up with love.
Since I have done you no favor,
For whose sake do you shed these tears?
Scrambling like mischievous children,
Trying to break my whip, to slash my stirrups –
By the roadside, that pair of stone men:
How many governors have they seen depart?
If they knew what was happening, how they'd laugh,
Clapping their hands till their hat strings snapped!

(43:18/12a)

In the opening lines, the poet points out that, since "My life is made of sojourns only," separation is inevitable, and the sorrow which separation occasions may be said to be an ever-present element in human life. But if "separation follows us everywhere," then is it not foolish to allow one's emotions to become so bound up with the occasion? In pointing out the omnipresence of sorrow, he urges a way to escape it. In the lines that follow he deliberately adopts a cold attitude, denying that he has done anything to win the affection of the people, scolding them for trying impetuously to prevent his departure by breaking his whip or attempting to cut his stirrups. In the closing lines he returns once more to the theme of the frequency of parting, pointing to the stone figures by the roadside and imagining how many times in the past they have witnessed such a scene of the departure of a governor. If they were aware of what went on around them, they would surely laugh uproariously at the foolishness of human beings in behaving in this fashion over something as frequent and inevitable as separation. The poet no doubt felt deep regret at leaving the people of Hsü-chou, among whom he had lived for over two years. But, at least on the surface of the poem, none of this appears; he merely points to the ubiquitous nature of sorrow, and advises us not to become preoccupied with it.

This is the second stage of Su's new, broad-visioned philosophy, by which he proposes to transcend sorrow. But the poem quoted above also reveals a very important mode of thinking which makes it representative of the third state of Su's philosophy. I am referring to the view which sees man's life as a thing of long duration. This outlook is revealed in the third line: "My life is made of sojourns only," which in the original is in simile form, literally, "My life is like sojourns only."

True, on the surface the line says nothing about life being long. The surface meaning is that life is a thing of doubt and uncertainty, like so many inn stops along a road. But beneath the surface there exists an awareness of the long time-span of human life. If there were no such awareness, then the following line, "Is this the first time I've had to take leave?" with its sense of an almost endless succession of partings stretching out of the past and into the future, would be impossible to imagine.

If we look back now at the first two stages of Su's philosophy we will see that the view of cyclical change which appears in the first stage, and the recognition of the omnipresence of sorrow in human life which appears in the second stage, both imply a consciousness of the long duration of human life. But this consciousness is first clearly stated in the line, "My life is made of sojourns only."

This is not the only poem in which the poet employs this line; it is to be found in many places in his works, as is the similar line in the poem to his brother, quoted earlier: "Our lives are like wind-blown tumbleweed." These two similes, the brief sojourn and the wind-blown tumbleweed, in addition to expressing the uncertainty of life, often imply the unspoken premise that man's life is of long duration. For example, in the poem called "Passing the Huai," which was written when the poet had been released from prison and was on his way to exile in Huang-chou, we find the following lines which imply that, because life is nothing but a long series of ups and downs, one's destination can never be fixed:

> My life is made of sojourns only,
> And I never get to choose the place I'm to go.

> (43:20/4a)

Or, in a poem written to the rhymes of a poem by his friend Wang Chin-ch'ing, in which the poet, after his return to political power, reminisces over his period of exile in Huang-chou, we read:

> My life is made of sojourns only;
> What is good luck, what is bad?
> Better to forget them both.
> Who can recapture last night's dream?
>
> (43:29/18b)

The view of cyclical change, the alternation of good luck and bad, demands a long period of time in order to be conceivable.

Another example is to be found in a poem written during his exile on Hainan Island and employing the same rhymes as T'ao Yüan-ming's poem entitled "Imitating the Ancients":

> My life is made of sojourns only;
> What shall I point to and call my house?
>
> (43:42/8a)

Because life is of such long duration, one may come to realize that any place is home.

The last example I shall cite is from a poem written when the poet had left Hainan Island and passed through Yü-ku-t'ai in Kiangsi on his way north:

> My life is made of sojourns only;
> The peaks and the sea – those were pleasure trips too.
>
> (43:45/2b)

The "peaks and the sea" refer respectively to his places of exile in Hui-chou and Hainan Island. Looking back on it, the poet now sees that his exile too was only one small incident in a long life crowded with incident, just another "pleasure trip."

This view, which sees man's life as a period of long duration, is original with Su; or, if it is not actually original with him, he used it to create a new era of poetry, for such a view had never been common in the poetry of earlier times. Until Su's time, it had been customary, on the contrary, to emphasize the brevity and fleeting quality of man's life.

As evidence we may point to the fact that the sojourn simile is never used in earlier poetry in the way in which Su used it. The simile itself is by no means original with Su, but is very old in Chinese poetry.

Su Tung-p'o's two poems on the Spring Festival Day, in the poet's hand-writing. From a collection in the Osaka City Museum.

A postscript to Su Tung-p'o's poems, composed and written by Huang T'ing-chien.

Four poems by Fan Ch'eng-ta in his own calligraphy,
as engraved on stone by the monk to whom he wrote them.
From an ink rubbing in the Imperial Palace, Tokyo.

Before his time, however, it was employed rather to emphasize the brief duration of man's life and the swiftness with which he moves toward death. It is found first in the twelfth of the anonymous "Nineteen Old Poems" which date from the first or second century A.D.:

> Man's life is brief as a sojourn;
> His years lack the firmness of metal or stone.[1]
>
> (12:3/56)

Ts'ao P'i (188–226) used the simile in his poem in folk-song style entitled *Shan-tsai-hsing*, again probably to emphasize the brevity of life:

> Man's life is like a sojourn;
> With so many sorrows, what can he do?
>
> (13:1/126)

Chu Yi, a scholar of the Southern Sung, in the first *chüan* of his *Yi-chüeh-liao tsa-chi*, has noted the sources from which Su Tung-p'o took his allusions and figures of speech. On the sojourn simile, he points to the following lines in a poem entitled "Thoughts on the Times" by Po Chü-i:

> How long is the life of man?
> He is in the world for a sojourn only.   (14:4712–3)

and those in a poem by the same poet called "Autumn Mountain":

> Man's life lasts no time at all,
> Like a sojourn between heaven and earth."
>
> (14:4719)

All of these examples obviously place emphasis upon the brevity of life.

But Su, while employing the same simile, invested it with a new meaning. What he did represents not only a shift in the meaning of the simile, but in the whole attitude toward human life. It is hardly necessary to add that the attitude which emphasizes the length of human life will be less productive of sorrow and despair, and more productive of hope, than one which emphasizes the brevity of life. True, Su sees life as a period which is full of ups and downs. But it is precisely

[1] Cf. also the passage in the *Lun heng* by Wang Ch'ung (AD 27–97?): "Life is a sojourn, death a return." *Lun heng* 5/6a, SPTK [Tr.].

because it is long that it is so marked by fluctuations. And when one is conscious of this lengthy and fluctuating character, it becomes more foolish than ever to allow oneself to think only of the sorrow which occurs during the low points. One must learn to put faith in the future.

We find this view of the length and changing quality of life clearly and logically stated in Su's works. But even where it is not explicitly stated, it seems always to underlie his poetry. We feel its presence, for example, in the famous poem in seven-character regulated verse written when the poet was en route by water from the capital to Hangchow. It bears the heading, "Passed the place where the Ying River enters the Huai, and for the first time saw the mountains along the Huai. Today we reached Shou-chou."

> I travel day and night toward the Yangtze and the sea.
> Maple leaves, reed flowers – fall has endless sights.
> On the broad Huai I can't tell if the sky is near or far;
> Green hills keep rising and falling with the boat.
> Shou-chou – already I see the white stone pagoda,
> Though short oars haven't brought us round Yellow Grass Hill.
> Waves calm, wind mild – I look for the landing.
> My friends have stood a long time in twilight mist.*   (43:6/24a)

Already in the opening lines we have a sense of life as a journey, as a thing of length and duration. In the lines that follow, the sky, whose distance it is impossible to discern, may be intended as a symbol of some aspect of man's life; the rising and falling of the green hills are surely meant to symbolize the up-and-down quality of life. After describing the circuitous course which the boat must take to reach its destination, the poet concludes on a note of expectation and quiet joy as he imagines how his friends, not yet in sight, have been standing waiting for him in the twilight mist.

Su Tung-p'o's philosophy for the transcendence of sorrow, the first three stages of which I have described above, reaches its culmination in the fourth stage. This culmination is to be found in the view that, if the outward process of life is characterized by a continuing series of ups and downs, then man's true inner life must lie in a continued resistance. This does not necessarily mean that one struggles against the ups and downs. The act of resignation may also be regarded as a kind of resistance exercised by the human will.

An early expression of this idea is to be found in the opening lines of "Beginning of Autumn: A Poem to Send to Tzu-yu," which the poet wrote during his period of exile in Huang-chou:

> The hundred rivers day and night flow on,
> We and all things following:
> Only the heart remains unmoved,
> Clutching the past.   (43:22/7b)

The same idea is clearly expressed in a poem written in 1097, during his second period of exile, when he was ordered to move from Hui-chou to the Island of Hainan. In five-character old form, it too is addressed to his brother Tzu-yu and begins as follows:

> I've had a lot of trouble from the time I was young,
> Dodging and threading my way through life.
> A hundred years aren't easy to live out;
> We must draw the strong bow inch by inch.
> I'm old – what is left to say?
> Honor and shame mean nothing now.
> I face the single road to nirvana;
> Wherever else I look, the way is blocked.   (43:41/4b)

Here the term "hundred years" applied to man's life clearly describes the sense of life's duration, while the metaphor of drawing a stiff bow expresses the exertion and resistance with which life must be lived. In the lines that follow the poet's nerve seems to fail him, and he speaks somewhat despairingly. But later on in the poem, we once more find such lines as the following:

> This parting, how's it worth talking about?
> My life surely won't come to an end yet!

A final example is to be found in a poem written in the summer of 1101, just before the poet's death. In five-character regulated verse, it is the second of two poems entitled "Following the Rhymes of Chiang

Hui-shu." It was written when he was traveling home along the Yangtze from his place of exile in the south.

> Bell and drum on the south river bank:
> Home! I wake startled from a dream.
> Drifting clouds – so the world shifts;
> Lone moon – such is the light of my mind.
> Rain drenches down as from a tilted basin;
> Poems flow out like water spilled.
> The two rivers vie to send me off;
> Beyond treetops I see the slant of a bridge.*
>
> (43:45/13ª)

In the opening couplet the poet wakes startled from a dream — a dream which in a larger sense is symbolic of the whole astonishing up-and-down course of his life. In the couplet that follows, in the contrast between the shifting clouds of the world and the steady brightness of the moon, he gives precise expression to the pride of a man who has resisted and overcome his environment. Wang Ying-lin, an eminent scholar of the end of the Southern Sung period, in his *K'un-hsüeh chi-wen*, comments upon this second couplet; "T'ung-p'o in his late years achieved great profundity" (27:18/12b). After a reference to the poet's unflagging creativity, the poem returns to a contemplation of the natural scene, ending with a delicate contrast between the rolling rivers and the static lines of the bridge seen above the tops of the trees.

I have attempted to outline the process by which Su Tung-p'o transcended sorrow. In the discussion of the line, "My life is a sojourn only," I have drawn gratefully upon the study by Yamamoto Kazuyoshi, "Some Remarks on the Poetry of Su Shih." [2] Certain aspects of my discussion may be based upon rather arbitrary judgments, but the correctness of my general conclusion is borne out, I believe, by the fact that, in spite of the extreme fluctuations of fortune to which the poet was subjected during his lifetime, his 2400 poems contain almost no works that are wholly sorrowful in tone. As case in point I will cite a poem written near the end of 1079 to say farewell to his brother. The poet was in prison under accusation of "slandering the Emperor," and fully expected to die. It is in seven-character regulated verse.

[2] *Journal of Chinese Literature*, 13:76–91 (October 1960).

Under the heaven of our holy ruler, all things turn to spring,
But I in dark ignorance have destroyed myself.
Before my hundred years are past, I'm called to settle up;
My leaderless family, ten mouths, must be your worry now.
Bury me anywhere on the green hills
And another year in night rain grieve for me alone.
Let us be brothers in lives and lives to come,
Mending then the bonds that this world breaks.*   (43:19/28b)

The poem is one of great sorrow, not surprisingly in view of the circumstances under which it was composed. Even so, there is a suggestion of hope, though it must wait until the next world for fulfillment. And although the word "to grieve," so rare in Su's poetry, appears here, it is interesting to note that it is applied not to the poet himself but to his brother.

This mood of sorrow did not last, however, for shortly after the poem quoted above was written, on the 28th day of the 12th month, after a hundred days in prison, the poet was set free. The following poem celebrates his release in terms of outspoken boldness. As I have already mentioned in the Introduction, it is in the same form and follows the same rhymes as the poem of sorrow quoted above, a fact that lends emphasis to the dramatic change of mood.

A hundred days, free to go, and it's almost spring;
For the years left, pleasure will be my chief concern.
Out the gate, I do a dance, wind blows my face;
Our galloping horses race along as magpies cheer.
I face the wine cup and it's all a dream,
Pick up a poem brush, already inspired.
Why try to fix the blame for trouble past?
Years now I've stolen posts I never should have had.*
(43:19/29b)

For the purpose of comparison I shall quote here a poem written under circumstances rather similar to those of Su's prison poem above. It is by the T'ang poet Han Yü and was written when he was on his way into exile in 819 after incurring the imperial wrath because of his attack on Buddhism expressed in his famous "Memorial on the Buddha Bone." Like Su's poem, it is seven-character regulated verse. It bears the title "Written on my way into exile when I reached the Lan-t'ien Pass and shown to my brother's grandson Hsiang." Hsiang had accompanied the poet as far as the Lan-t'ien Pass, south of Ch'ang-an.

> One document at dawn, submitted to the nine-tiered palace;
> By evening, banished to Ch'ao-chou eight thousand li away.
> For our holy ruler I longed to drive away the evil;
> What thought for this old body, for the few years remaining?
> Clouds blanket the Ch'in Range – which way is home?
> Snow blocks the Lan Pass – my horse will not go on.
> You must have some purpose, coming so far with me:
> Be kind and gather up my bones from the shores of the fetid river.
>
> (14:3859–60)

Like Su, Han Yü had resigned himself to the thought of death, and his poem is given up to sadness. The clouds of the Ch'in Range, the snow in the Lan-t'ien Pass, everything that he sees, serves only to deepen his sorrow. But, unlike Su, who imagines himself being buried somewhere "on the green hills," Han Yü can only visualize his bones being left to rot by the malarial rivers of Ch'ao-chou far to the south and begs his kinsman to rescue them from that fate.

Su Tung-p'o did more than simply transcend his own personal sorrow; he initiated a new era in the history of Chinese poetry. The preoccupation with sorrow which had become a habit with the poets of earlier ages was brought to an end by his efforts, and poetry was led into the direction of a more hopeful view of life. Su's admirers in later centuries have loved him for his largeness and freedom of spirit, and his detractors have criticized him for the almost excessive ease with which his poetry flows along. But whatever they have thought of him, the poets who lived after Su Tung-p'o gave far less space in their songs to the despair and sorrow of life than those who had lived before him, and this fact was the direct result of the revolution which he had brought about in the tenor of Chinese poetry.

Future historians of literature and philosophy will some day, it is to be hoped, make an exhaustive study of the epoch-making nature of Su Tung-p'o's literary works. When they do, they will have to give careful attention to one aspect of his personality in particular: the great breadth of his love. He was no political planner like Wang An-shih, but he had an innate love for the common people. It may be seen, for example, in the following poem written in 1071 when the poet was vice-governor of Hangchow. In five-character old form, it describes how the poet was kept late at his office on New Year's Eve by criminal cases. According to custom, cases involving the death penalty had to be settled before the New Year, which marked the beginning of spring.

New Year's Eve – you'd think I could go home early
But official business keeps me.
I hold the brush and face them with tears:
Pitiful convicts in chains,
Little men who tried to fill their bellies,
Fell into the law's net, don't understand disgrace.
And I? In love with a meager stipend
I hold on to my job and miss the chance to retire.
Do not ask who is foolish or wise;
All of us alike scheme for a meal.
The ancients would have freed them a while at New Year's –
Would I dare do likewise? I am silent with shame.*

(43:32/31a)

When the poet compares himself to the condemned prisoners and tells us, "Do not ask who is foolish or wise," he is not, I believe, speaking as a member of the ruling class who feels a certain tenderness toward his charges. He himself often denied that he belonged to the elite and expressed the desire to live the life of an ordinary citizen. When he was exiled to Huang-chou, he lived among farmers and actually became a farmer himself, working a plot of land at a place called Tung-p'o, or Eastern Slope. The following poem, the fifth of eight entitled "Eastern Slope," gives a glimpse of his life at that time. It is five-character old form.

A good farmer hates to wear out the land;
I'm lucky this plot was ten years fallow.
It's too soon to count on mulberries;
My best bet is a crop of wheat.
I planted seed and within the month

Dirt on the rows was showing green.
An old farmer warned me,
Don't let seedlings shoot up too fast!
If you want plenty of dumpling flour
Turn a cow or sheep in here to graze.
Good advice – I bowed my thanks;
I won't forget you when my belly's full.*

(43:21/1b)

He hoped to become a farmer once more at the time of his second exile in Hainan Island, as may be seen in the following poem dating from that period, though he was unable to realize his desire. In five-character old poem form, it is called "Buying Rice." As the poet buys rice and other necessities in the market place, he images how happy he would be if he could have a plot of land and grow his own food.

I buy rice and bundles of firewood,
Each commodity at its proper stall.
But getting them like this without plowing or gathering,
Though I fill my belly, the flavor is thin.
Bowing twice, I'll beg the lord of the land
Please to let me have a plot of ground.
I know where I was wrong, I laugh at past dreams;
If I work for my food, I need feel no shame.
Spring seedlings – when will they bloom?
Summer barngrass – its seeds are ripe by now!
Fondly I will stroke the plow and share –
Who understands what it would mean to me?

(43:41/16a)

The principal fault of Su Tung-p'o's poetry is that he often wrote with an ease and facility that bordered on carelessness. In the poem quoted on page 116 above we have already encountered a description of the facility with which he composed: "Poems flow out like water spilled"; and in another poem he writes,

A new poem is like a crossbow pellet;
Once it's left the hand it never stops a moment.

(43:19/3b)

He certainly did not belong to the painstaking, hard-working category of poets. His manner of composition was an expression of the freedom of his mind and of his talent. But although he himself was not the hard-working type, he could appreciate the worth of the man who was perhaps the hardest-working poet of the past, Tu Fu, and, along with Wang An-shih, strived to win for Tu Fu the recognition he deserved.

As I have mentioned in the Introduction, Su Tung-p'o composed poems to the rhymes of all of T'ao Yüan-ming's poems, completing the task during his years of exile in Hainan. This feat, too, is an expression of the overflow of energy and talent which characterized his work. I shall quote an example of T'ao Yüan-ming's poetry and the poem which Su wrote to match it. T'ao Yüan-ming's poem is the third of his twenty poems entitled "Drinking Wine," in five-character lines.

> A thousand years the Way's been lost;
> Men are stingy with their hearts.
> They have wine but they're unwilling to drink;
> They think of nothing but worldly fame.
> What's so precious about this body of ours?
> Is it not the fact that it's alive?
> One life – how long does it last?
> Swift as a bolt of lightning it passes.
> Within the press of a hundred years,
> What will you do with this fame of yours?
>
> (11:6/472)

The following is Su's poem, which employs the same rhyme words. The "refined gentlemen south of the Yangtze" are T'ao Yüan-ming's contemporaries of the Eastern Chin dynasty, which had its capital at Nanking.

> The Way is lost, and men have lost themselves;
> Words spoken now are never from the heart.
> The refined gentlemen south of the Yangtze
> In the midst of drunkenness still sought fame.
> Yüan-ming alone was pure and true,
> Living his life in talk and laughter.
> He was like a bamboo before the wind,
> Swaying and bending, all its leaves atremble,

> Some facing up, some down, each a different shape –
> When he'd had his wine, the poems wrote themselves.
>
> (43:35/10a)

The last line probably refers less to T'ao Yüan-ming's way of writing poetry than it does to that of Su Tung-p'o himself.

Wang An-shih, in spite of his good intentions, was never popular with the common people of his time. Su Tung-p'o, by contrast, seems to have been loved by all who knew him. There must have been something very different in the manner of the two men. Su's poetic follower, the Buddhist priest Ts'an-liao, wrote the following poem after Su's death. In seven-character *chüeh-chü* form, it is entitled "Poem Written in Memory of My Teacher Tung-p'o."

> When with tall hat and firm baton he stood in council,
> The crowds were awed at the dignity of the statesman in him.
> But when in cloth cap he strolled with cane and sandals,
> He greeted little children with gentle smiles.   (48:11/5b)

Ts'an-liao was also acquainted with Wang An-shih. For the sake of comparison, I shall quote a poem which he wrote on visiting the Ting-lin Temple where Wang An-shih, referred to here by his title Duke Ching, used to walk. In the same form as the poem above, it is called "Visiting the Ting-lin Temple and Paying My Respects to the Portrait of Duke Ching."

> Old trees, green rattan, one trail winding through;
> Our Duke in days past would wander here.
> Under the lonely roof, I look at his portrait:
> The hero's air, the noble pose, impressive still.
>
> (48:7/7a)

Huang T'ing-chien (1045–1105)

Su Tung-p'o, with his great tolerance and breadth of personality, attracted many young poets to his side. Of particular note among these are Huang T'ing-chien (1045–1105), Chang Lei (1054–1114), Ch'ao Pu-chih (1053–1110), and Ch'in Kuan (1049–1101), often referred to as the "Four Scholars of the Su School." A fifth poet, Ch'en Shih-tao (1053–1101), became a disciple of Su's at a somewhat later date. In the number of his disciples, Su's case contrasts with that of Wang An-shih, who had only one disciple whose works have survived, Wang Ling (1032–1095).

Among these disciples of Su Tung-p'o, the most important as a poet is Huang T'ing-chien, and in fact the names of Su and Huang are often paired. Huang was a native of Yü-chang, the present-day Nan-ch'ang, in the province of Kiangsi, and became the founder of the so-called Chiang-hsi (Kiangsi) School of poetry.

The association between Su and Huang began in 1078, when Huang presented to Su his "Two Old-Poetry Form Poems for Su Tzu-chan" (Tzu-chan was Su Tung-p'o's polite name); Su was forty-three and Huang was thirty-four. Su, whose own activities were so varied, was much impressed with the work of this young man who devoted himself solely to the practice of poetry, and declared that Huang's poetry was superior to his own. In this respect their relationship resembles that which existed between Ou-yang Hsiu and Mei Yao-ch'en. Eight years after Huang T'ing-chien became associated with Su, in 1086, we find Su declaring as a joke that, although his own couplets are the wonder of the age, "they are actually imitations of the T'ing-chien style." It was around this time that Su succeeded in securing a position for his disciple as an editor engaged in the task of preparing the official account of the reign of the recently deceased Emperor Shen-tsung.

Huang lived up to Su's expectations, and his works are more intense, as poetry, than those of his teacher. His temperament, too, differed from that of his teacher, his introversion contrasting with Su's candor. In his poetry he sought to achieve a feeling of tense stillness. Here, for example, is a poem written in 1071, before he had become associated with Su. In it the poet describes the experience of listening to his father-in-law's younger sister play the *ch'in*, or horizontal lute. The poem is in old form, with a mixture of seven- and five-character lines.

> The moon is bright, the river still. When all is quiet,
> My aunt spreads her sleeves and strikes the pawlonia lute.
> Men of long ago are gone, but their music is here;
> I seem to hear echoes of the Odes and Hymns.

A subtle touch is not easy to acquire;
A good listener is hard to find,
As rare as the udumbara
Blooming once in three thousand years.
We forget our own thoughts and those of the lute;
It's as though her ten fingers did not touch the strings.
Still as the triple abyss, her Zen mind is dumb,
A deep valley where pure winds mingle lightly.
Who says strings cannot compare to flutes?
I've forgotten words and found my true nature.
She stops. Beyond the window, the moon sinks into the river.
The ten thousand pipes are empty, the seven strings subside.

(37:*wai-shih* 2/4a)

The "Odes and Hymns" is a reference to the music, lost long ago, which was used to accompany the Odes and Hymns sections of the *Book of Odes*. The term "triple abyss" in line eleven derives from *Chuang Tzu* (section 7): "The abyss has nine names and I have shown him three." Huang T'ing-chien was even more interested in the teachings of Zen Buddhism than Su Tung-p'o. Line fourteen is an allusion to *Chuang Tzu* (section 26): "Words exist because of meaning; once you've gotten the meaning, you can forget the words." The last line also contains an allusion to the famous description in *Chuang Tzu* (section 2) of the "piping of earth," when "ten thousand hollows begin crying wildly . . . And when the fierce wind has passed on, then all the hollows are empty again."

Huang's introverted personality is reflected in the extreme attention which he gave to the selection of words, an attention which at times led him into obscurity. In this he is totally unlike Su, whose genius on occasion found almost too facile an expression. The poem by Huang T'ing-chien quoted above is not a good example of this obscurity, though the use of the verb *ting* in the last line — "the seven strings subside" — is peculiar enough in this sense.

Again, Huang's dislike for the commonplace led him to avoid both the diction and the modes of expression of earlier poets, and to seek to discover poetry in the minor happenings of the every day world. The poem in five-character old-form entitled "To go with the Bamboo,

Rocks, and Herd Boy" serves as an example. Su Tung-p'o had done a small painting of rocks and bamboo, to which Li Kung-lin had added the figure of a herd boy; Huang then supplied this poem to accompany the picture. It was written in 1088, when Huang was working under Su in the Han-lin Academy.

> Over in the field, the little crags and peaks,
> A quiet bamboo grove, green on green leaning:
> The herd boy with a three-foot whip
> Drives these sad old oxen before him.
> The rocks – how I love them!
> Don't let the oxen sharpen their horns there!
> Or if you let them sharpen their horns,
> Don't let them fight – they'll ruin my bamboo!
>
> (37:9/12b)

One can imagine the small painting, with its little rocks and quickly sketched bamboo which Su had produced, a miniature world with its "green on green leaning." The admonitions to the herd boy are probably intended as a humorous gibe at Li Kung-lin for adding the figure of the herd boy to the painting.

The poet whom Huang respected most was Tu Fu. Huang outdid even Wang An-shih and Su Tung-p'o in his admiration for the poet and his efforts to see that Tu Fu's work was properly appreciated. In his late years, Huang was exiled to Ch'ien-chou and Jung-chou in present-day Szechwan at the same time that his teacher, Su Tung-p'o, was exiled to the southeast. Huang was a noted calligrapher and at this time wrote out the texts of all the poems composed by Tu Fu during his period of wandering in Szechwan and had them engraved on stone, as he himself records in his "Preface to the Engravings of Tu Tzu-mei's Pa-Shu Poems" (59:16/34a).

What attracted him was Tu Fu's introspective nature. He shared with him a fondness for polished diction and the careful observation of the minutest changes in the natural world. Huang was recognized by his contemporaries as the most assiduous student of Tu Fu's art, and in fact was looked upon as the Tu Fu of his day. And yet in the end Huang's poetry does not resemble the earlier poet's — in fact, it is totally different, because Huang made no effort to equal the breadth of Tu Fu's passion.

Earlier poets have given frank expression to their passion — even the introverted Tu Fu — but this type of emotional expression Huang T'ing-chien deliberately avoided. He not only scorned it as childish and even primitive, but actively condemned it because he felt that it interfered with the careful observation of the minute and subtle changes in the world. One's first impression on reading his poetry is that of coldness and dryness; he avoided and forcibly repressed any expression of genuine feeling in his poetry. Perhaps the only poem of his which comes near to describing real passion is that written in his late years at Yi-chou in Kwangsi entitled "Inscribed on the Back of the Stele at Mo-ya" (37:20/2a).

In this sense Huang's writing represents a kind of heresy directed at the poetry of previous ages, or at the common-sense conception of poetry prevalent in any age, namely, that it is first of all an expression of feeling. This heretical strain is present to some degree throughout Sung poetry, or at least the poetry written from Mei Yao-ch'en's time on. This seemingly antipoetic quality has already been suggested earlier in Ou-yang Hsiu's comparison of Mei Yao-ch'en's poetry to olives which are bitter when first tasted, and it is this quality which was most carefully cultivated by Huang T'ing-chien.

This does not mean that Huang was a man devoid of feeling. Like his teacher Su Tung-p'o, he was affectionate in nature and had an innate love for the city people about him. Elsewhere I have discussed this trait as it appears in the poem in which he explains how, had he failed in the civil service examination, he would have liked to open a small medicine shop and help cure the ills of his fellow townsmen. The following poem illustrates the same point. Written in 1087 and called "A City Hermit of Ch'en-liu," it is accompanied by an introduction which describes the subject of the poem, a barber of the city of Ch'en-liu. Over forty and without a wife, the barber goes about the city streets carrying a little girl of seven on his shoulders — not his own child but an orphan whom he has adopted. As he goes along he makes a noise with the huge tweezers that are the mark of his trade. With the day's earnings he buys wine and, sticking a flower in his hair, plays on a long horizontal flute. In such a life, the poet adds, real happiness is to be found. The poem is in five-character regulated verse.

> A man of the market place with mind like a pearl –
> I've walked many streets but never found one before.
> The pretty little girl rides his shoulders;
> They happen to go through life together.
> The frost-white razor is there – it nourishes the living;
> The clear mirror, empty, looks at many men.
> And from time to time he has his wine;
> Twanging the tweezers, he says goodby to the flying swan.
>
> (37:6/8a)

The last line is an allusion to Hsi K'ang, poet and philosopher of the third century A.D., and one of the Seven Sages of the Bamboo Grove, who, it is said,

> With his eyes said goodby to the flying swan,
> And with his hand plucked the five strings.
>
> (13:4/206)

The old barber, as much a philosopher as the celebrated Hsi K'ang, sounds his tweezers instead of a lute. In China the huge tweezers and the twanging sound they make have continued until recent times to be the trademark of the itinerant barber.

Huang embraced the same philosophy of life as his teacher Su — a philosophy of resistance that may be seen in the following poem. It was written in 1100, when the poet was fifty-six and had been granted permission to leave his place of exile in Jung-chou. It is in five-character old form and was written to the same rhyme as a poem by someone named Yang Ming-shu who had come to see him off.

> Pine and cypress growing in the river valley
> Sit staring at the autumn of grass and trees;
> Metal and stone there beneath the waves
> Gaze up at the flow of the ten thousand things.
> Let the jolly bustler do his bustling,
> Let the timid moaner make his moan.
> Only look a hundred years from now –
> It won't be lords and nobles whose names are handed down!
>
> (37:14/3b)

The "pine and cypress" which watch complacently while the other trees and grasses shed their leaves, as well as the "metal and stone" which similarly resist change, are symbols of the poet himself. Wang Ying-lin singled out the couplet beginning "Metal and stone" for special praise, along with the couplet in Su Tung-p'o's poem quoted earlier (p. 116):

> Drifting clouds – so the world shifts;
> Lone moon – such is the light of my mind.

Though Huang T'ing-chien was twice exiled because of his disagreements with the New Laws party, we find no tearful laments among his poetic works, another point in which he resembles his teacher Su.

Huang T'ing-chien came nearest, among all his contemporaries, to being completely the artist. His poems, like those of his spiritual forefather in the new movement of Sung poetry, Mei Yao-ch'en, are focused upon the details of everyday life, though he perhaps realized more clearly than Mei Yao-ch'en the significance which the minor ups and downs of daily life have for man's life as a whole, and sought to give artistic shape to them. Like Mei Yao-ch'en, who boasted that he was the first man to write a poem on the subject of lice, Huang T'ing-chien also treated subjects that had never been treated before. Such, for example, are his poems on the *la-mei*, or "wax plum," whose delicate blossoms seem to be fashioned out of wax, and the tree with little white flowers known as *pai-fan-hua*, or "white alum flower"; both of these he employed as symbols. Here is one of his poems entitled "Wax Plum," in five-character old-form.

> Gold buds still barred against spring cold,
> The fragrance that unnerves men not yet spread;
> Though you have not the face of peach or damson,
> Your character too is far from shallow.   (37:5/6b)

I shall close this discussion of Huang T'ing-chien with three poems that will, I hope, help to illustrate the qualities mentioned above. The first, "Song of the Clear River," in seven-character old-style, was written when Huang was very young.

River gulls bob and toss in reed-flower autumn;
Eighty-year-old fisherman, not a worry in a hundred:
By clear dawn he works the scull, picking lotus pods;
By evening sun he hauls in the net, letting the boat drift.
His little boys are learning to fish – not bad at all;
His old woman, white-haired, has pleasures still ahead.
The whole family, wine-drowsy, sleep beneath the thatch,
Their boat on the cold sand where night tides run out.

(37:*wai-shih* 1/5a)

The second, seven-character *chüeh-chü*, bears the title "Sixth month, Seventeenth Day: Noonday Nap." "Sea-blue Isle" is another name for the mythical island of the immortal spirits in the Eastern Sea.

Straw-hatted, black-booted, amid red dust,
I thought I saw the paired white birds of the Sea-blue Isle.
The horse chomping dried bean hulls made a noise by my noonday pillow;
In my dream it turned to wind and rain; waves rose up on the river.

(37:11/8a)

The last, also a seven-character *chüeh-chü*, is entitled "For my nephew Shih who will join his father Chih-ming on the trip by boat."

Why push off from sandy banks and study how to catch fish?
Why rig the stern reel with a hundred-fathom line?
In clear rivers wash your feet, sitting under the porthole.
Swallow-time days are long now – just right for reading books.

(37:13/5a)

As a postscript to the sections on Su Tung-p'o and Huang T'ing-chien, it may be mentioned that these were the two poets most enthusiastically read by the so-called Gozan, or "Five Temple," Zen monks of Japan during the Kamakura and Muromachi periods. Many editions of their works produced in Japan are still extant, as well as the texts with explications in Japanese script known as *shō*. These in time came to exert an influence upon the Japanese poet Bashō, who spoke of "the freshness of Su and the strangeness of Huang" in his *Oi no obumi*, and in his *Minomushi no setsubatsu*. The phrase was not original with Bashō but derives from a remark by Ch'en Shih-tao (see below) quoted in a miscellany entitled *Jade Chips from the Poets* (chüan

12). This work, the *Shih-jen yü-hsieh*, is a collection of remarks and anecdotes about poetry compiled around the end of the Southern Sung. Ch'en's original remark was that "Wang . . . [An-shih] did it with skill, Su . . . did it with freshness, and Huang . . . did it with strangeness." A Japanese woodblock edition of *Jade Chips from the Poets* was published in 1639, and Bashō probably picked up the phrase from it.

Ch'en Shih-tao (1053–1102)

The name of this last disciple of Su Tung-p'o is often mentioned with that of Huang T'ing-chien. Like his friend Huang, Ch'en Shih-tao was a native of Kiangsu (from Hsü-chou), and likewise devoted his fullest attention to poetry. "I give all the energies of this life to poetry," he wrote, and Huang wrote of him that "he would shut his gate and search for couplets" (37:14/9b). Exactly what Huang meant by this is explained by a passage in the *Chu-tzu yü-lei* (ch. 140). There Chu Hsi remarks that if Ch'en Shih-tao happened to think of a good line when he was out walking, he would go home, get in bed, and, pulling the covers over him like a sick man, would lie there for days at a time mulling over the line.

Ch'en Shih-tao, like Huang T'ing-chien, was an admirer and imitator of Tu Fu. In attempting to carry on the style of the earlier poet, however, he was less one-sided than Huang T'ing-chien, and his imitations give a truer reflection of the real Tu Fu. Near the beginning of the twelve-*chüan* collection of his poetry entitled *Hou-shan shih-chi*, we find the following five-character old-poem called "Parting from My Three Children." It is included in almost all anthologies of Sung poetry and is a good illustration of Ch'en writing in the Tu Fu manner. It was written in 1084 when the poet, because of poverty, was obliged to send off his wife and three children to live with his father-in-law, an official in Szechwan. The poet's description of his feelings as he sees his family off is obviously influenced by Tu Fu's descriptions of familial affection.

> In death man and wife share the same grave,
> But poverty parts a father and his sons.
> Under Heaven can there be such a thing?

I have heard of it once — now I see it.
The mother in front, three children behind:
I stare at them but cannot run after.
Ah-ah, what heartlessness,
To make me come to this!
My daughter has just begun to plait her hair
And knows the grief that comes when the living must part.
She leans on me and won't get up,
Afraid I will go away and leave her.
The older boy is learning to talk;
He tries to bow but can't manage his robe.
"Goodby, Papa!" he calls –
How can I listen to such words?
The little boy is in swaddling clothes;
His mother holds him tight with love.
Your crying voices are still in my ears.
What man can know how I feel?   (19:1/4b)

Ch'en wrote many poems in regulated-verse style, like that already quoted in the Introduction, undoubtedly out of a desire to follow the example of Tu Fu. In diction also he consciously imitated him. Finally, like a true heir of Tu Fu, he did not hesitate to express his sorrow openly. This is already evident from the poem just quoted. In the following poem in five-character regulated verse entitled "Cold Night" he explains the reason for this. The poem was written in 1100, when the poet had just been transferred from a post in his home region of Hsü-chou to another at Ti-chou in Shantung.

A long time in one place and I always think of moving;
Then I find the same trouble and regret having changed.
I raise the wick of the cold lamp but the flame is out;
I rake up what's left of the fire but it has turned to ash.
Icy water drips a while and then stops;
Windy blinds flap open and shut.
I know well enough what writing should avoid,
But thoughts come, bringing sadness with them.

                                                (19:11/22b)

Jen Yüan, in a note to this poem which was added shortly after Ch'en's death, cites the words of Wang An-shih already quoted, "Writing should particularly avoid too frequent sorrow," believing that Ch'en had this in mind when he composed the final couplet. In the original, the compounds *liu-chih* ("remain in one place"), *chien-yü* ("trouble, difficulty"), and *feng-lien* ("windy blinds") are all expressions which are found in Tu Fu's regulated-verse poems.

The idea that a poem should, among other things, be an expression of intellect, reached its point of widest acceptance in the work of Su Tung-p'o and Huang T'ing-chien. Sung poetry from their time on, as I shall show in the section that follows, sought more and more to return to the simple lyricism of the T'ang style. This tendency is already to be found in the work of Su Tung-p'o's disciples, as the poetry of Ch'en Shih-tao demonstrates. The men like Ch'en who sought to carry on the style of Tu Fu, however, succeeded in capturing his delicacy but not his grandeur, and their work is often marked by a certain fragility.

Ch'en Shih-tao died in the first year of Emperor Hui-tsung's reign, the same year in which his teacher Su Tung-p'o died, on a day that would fall early in 1102 by the Western calendar. He held a minor post as a proofreader in the state archives, and was ordered to attend the ceremony held at the open-air Altar of Heaven on the occasion of the winter solstice. He owned only one cloak, and wearing this, he stood through the long ceremony exposed to the night wind. His wife had gone to the home of a relative, the high official Chao T'ing-chih, to borrow another cloak, which she urged her husband to wear, but he declared that he would not put on the cloak of "a vile New Laws party man!" and went off to the ceremony shivering in his single cloak. He fell sick as a result and died on New Year's Eve. The account of his death is found in the *Chu-tzu yü-lei*, ch. 140.

In addition to Huang T'ing-chien and Ch'en Shih-tao, Su Tung-p'o had many other poet disciples and friends, among whom the most important are Ch'in Kuan, a native of Kiangsu; Chang Lei, also from Kiangsu; Ch'ao Pu-chih and his cousin Ch'ao Ch'ung-chih from Shan-tung; Su's cousin Wen T'ung, who was famous as a painter of bamboo; the celebrated painter Mi Fei; and the Buddhist priest Ts'an-liao. Among these, Ch'in Kuan, whose poem on "Country Life" has been quoted in the Introduction, excelled in poetry in the *tz'u* form and has therefore been highly regarded by literary historians of recent years. But his poetry has a kind of effeminate weakness to it, which led the Chin poet Yüan Hao-wen (1190–1257) to dub it "maiden's poetry." Through the influence of his teacher Su Tung-p'o he secured a post in the government and was exiled to the south when his teacher fell into disfavor. From this period on his poetry becomes noticeably maudlin. Whatever his poetic manner, Ch'in seems to have been entirely masculine in appearance, wearing a heavy beard that won him the nickname "Bearded Ch'in." Huang T'ing-chien has described his outgoing personality in the following line: "He would face his visitors and wield the brush; that was Ch'in Shao-yu (Ch'in Kuan)" (37:14/9b) — an interesting contrast to the introvert Ch'en Shih-tao who would "shut his gate and search for couplets." He seems to have been a highly talented member of the new bureaucratic class, and his ambitious and complex personality is reflected in his literary works.

Chapter Five

END OF THE NORTHERN SUNG AND

BEGINNING OF THE SOUTHERN SUNG

1100–1150

The Chiang-hsi School

In 1101 the great poet Su Tung-p'o, his period of banishment in Hainan ended, died at Ch'ang-chou on his way north. His death marks the end of an era. His disciples did not outlive him by long. Ch'in Kuan and Ch'en Shih-tao died in the same year as their teacher; Huang T'ing-chien died four years later, to be followed by Ch'ao Pu-chih in 1110, Su Tung-p'o's younger brother Su Ch'e in 1112, and Chang Lei in 1114.

The life of the Northern Sung regime was also drawing to a close. When Emperor Hui-tsung came to the throne he adopted, as we have seen, the era name *Chien-chung-ching-kuo* — "Rule of the Nation Based on the Mean" — which suggested that he would seek a compromise between the New Laws party and its opponents. But this era name was used for one year only, and the following year, 1102, a new era name, *Ch'ung-ning*, meaning "To Honor Ning," was adopted. "Ning" refers to the *Hsi-ning* period (1068–1077) and indicates that Emperor Hui-tsung intended to follow the policies adopted by his father, Emperor Shen-tsung, during the *Hsi-ning* period — that is, the reforms of the New Laws party. Wang An-shih's son-in-law, Ts'ai Pien, together with his older brother Ts'ai Ching, assumed power, and a list of the names of one hundred twenty men of the conservative party who were to be purged was drawn up and distributed to the provinces, together with orders that the list be carved in stone and set up in public places. Containing names of men like Ssu-ma Kuang, Su Tung-p'o, and

Ch'in Kuan, who were already dead, as well as such men as Huang T'ing-chien, who were still alive, it is known as the "stone list of the *Yüan-yu* era (1086–1093) party." Orders were also given that the publication of literary works by the men whose names appeared on the list was to be halted. A proposal was even put forward that the writing of poetry, because it was an art so closely associated with Su Tung-p'o and the other "evil ministers" of the *Yüan-yu* party, should be forbidden, but since Emperor Hui-tsung himself continued to write poetry, the proposal came to nothing.[1]

The leaders of the New Laws party, Ts'ai Ching and Ts'ai Pien, claimed that they were reviving the policies of Wang An-shih, but they failed to imitate Wang's scrupulous integrity and actually encouraged the young emperor in his extravagant ways. Emperor Hui-tsung is noted as a connoisseur and collector of antiques and works of art, and as a painter and calligrapher. Specimens of his painting and calligraphy (leaving aside for the moment the troublesome question of just which items are genuine), found their way to Japan, the calligraphy done in a delicate and distinctive manner known as "lean gold style"; a catalogue of the works in his collection, the *Po-ku-t'u*, is still in existence. He was also a music lover, and employed the famous writer of *tz'u* style songs, Chou Mei-ch'eng, as a member of his musical troup, the *Ta-sheng-fu*. He had a large garden constructed, known as *Ken-yüeh* (Mountain Peaks) or *Wan-sui-shan* (Ten Thousand Year Mountains) and ordered the wealthy families of the south to contribute trees and rocks from their own gardens. Rumor had it that he carried on a love affair with a famous courtesan of the capital, Li Shih-shih. The following poem by Emperor Hui-tsung, a seven-character *chüeh-chü* called "Palace Song," describes the ladies-in-waiting playing ball in the imperial gardens.

> West of the park, by the porch edge, the emerald moat is long;
> The tall bamboo is thick and leafy, its green shadows cool.
> In play they toss the water ball, seeing who can throw the farthest.
> A falling star – one dot – shines in the light of the waves.
>
> (45:1/9)

---

[1] See the sections on Emperor Hui-tsung, Chang Shun-min, and Ch'en Shih-tao in the *Sung-shih chi-shih*, or *Notes on Sung Poetry*.

The capital, Pien-ching, or K'ai-feng, having enjoyed peace for well over a hundred years, continued to live a life of vain splendor, a life recalled and recorded years later, after it had vanished, by Meng Yüan-lao in his *Tung-ching meng-hua lu*, or *A Journey in Memory to the Eastern Capital*. In the countryside, however, there was unrest, and groups of peasants were rising in revolt. The fortunes of one such group in Shantung, headed by the famous Sung Chiang, is described, with some fictionalization, in the novel *Shui-hu-chuan*, or *Water Margin*, and even the *Classified Sayings of Chu Hsi* contain remarks on the uprisings of this period.

The end came in 1126, twenty-five years after Emperor Hui-tsung ascended the throne. A little earlier, the non-Chinese state of Chin, an ally of the Sung, had overthrown the Sung's old enemy to the north, the state of Liao. In 1126, the armies of the Chin, claiming that the Chinese had failed to live up to their treaty, surrounded the capital and carried off Emperor Hui-tsung and his son, Emperor Ch'in-tsung, along with the women and treasures of the palace, to their stronghold in Manchuria. Emperor Hui-tsung died in confinement nine years later in the region called Wu-kuo-ch'eng in present-day Kirin, in northeast Manchuria. The following seven-character *chüeh-chü* was said to have been found inscribed on the wall of the lodge where he was confined.

> All night the west wind bangs the broken door;
> The lonely lodge is desolate, the single lamp dim.
> Hills of home – I turn to look three thousand miles away,
> But my eyes are blocked at the south horizon where no geese fly.
>
> (36:3a)

Wild geese have since early times been the traditional message-bearers in Chinese poetry and the symbol of communication.

Another son of Emperor Hui-tsung, known as Emperor Kao-tsung, became the first ruler of the Southern Sung. For a while he moved from place to place in the south, but later chose the city of Hangchow in Chekiang to be his capital. He reigned for thirty-six years. During the early years of his rule, the court was split over the question of whether to attack the Chin or to establish peaceful relations with it. After Prime Minister Ch'in Kuei, leader of the peace party, arranged the assassination of his opponent, General Yüeh Fei, a peace treaty was concluded with the Chin in 1141 and the strife within the southern court came to an end. Emperor Kao-tsung, like his father, was a skilled calligrapher, and his new capital, Hangchow, situated on the beautiful West Lake, was marked by an atmosphere of genial refinement. A seven-character *chüeh-chü* by a man named Kao Hsiao-chou describes a scene on West Lake where the Dragon Barge — the imperial barge — has been sailing during the afternoon:

> White boats with vermion blinds dazzle the light of the lake;
> On the far bank the Dragon Barge ties up in the evening sun.
> Today we laugh and play, and again tomorrow,
> Bringing Ching-lo here to Ch'ien-t'ang.   (60:71/20a)

Ching-lo is another name for Pien-ching, or K'ai-feng, the old Sung capital in the north; Ch'ien-t'ang is an alternate name for Hangchow. The poet boasts that all the glory of the old northern capital has been transferred to the new imperial residence in the south. But, although the emperor and his courtiers showed less and less interest in any attempt to regain control of the north, the capital of the nation continued, though only in name, to be the city of Pien-ching in the north, and Hangchow was referred to as *Hsing-tsai*, meaning "the place where the emperor is in residence." The exact date of the poem quoted above is unknown, and it may be from a somewhat later period, though it makes little difference, since the same air of merry-making continued to dominate the city of Hangchow "where the emperor is in residence" for the following century and a half, until the final downfall of the Sung dynasty in 1279.

During the latter years of Emperor Kao-tsung's reign, Wan-yen-liang, the ambitious emperor of the Chin, broke his treaty with the Sung and attempted an invasion of the south, drawn by the beauty and splendor of the city of Hangchow. When Emperor Kao-tsung had seen the invader repulsed in 1162 and peace restored to his "one-sided empire," he ceded the throne to his adopted son, who became Emperor Hsiao-tsung. It is said that, fearing for the safety of his own position, he had no desire to see his father, Emperor Hui-tsung, and his elder brother brought back from captivity in the enemy north.

The half-century of political weakness and misfortune was also a low point in the literary history of the age. There were no longer any great poets on the scene, only minor ones. The men who would become great in the following period, Lu Yu, Yang Wan-li, and Fan Ch'eng-ta, were still in their youth during the time of Emperor Kao-tsung and had not yet begun to reveal their talents.

Among their predecessors, the one whom the minor poets of this period sought most assiduously to imitate was Huang T'ing-chien. One of these minor poets, Lü Chü-jen (1137–1181), drew up a list showing the filiation of twenty-six of his contemporaries who were imitators of the Huang T'ing-chien style. Including such men as Ch'en Shih-tao and Ch'ao Ch'ung-chih who have already been mentioned, it was entitled *Filiation of the Chiang-hsi Poetry Group*. Chiang-hsi appears in the title because Huang T'ing-chien was a native of Chiang-hsi (Kiangsi), though a number of the men included in the list came from other parts of China. Lü Chü-jen was also said to have compiled a collection of the poetic works of these twenty-six men which ran to a hundred thirty-seven *chüan*, though it has not survived. The fact that so many of the poetic works of this period have been lost is due partly to the ravages of war and social disorder, but also in part, it would seem, to the fact that the court was torn by strife over the question of whether to make war on the Chin or to seek peaceful relations, and members of rival parties did their best to destroy the writings of their opponents.

The so-called Chiang-hsi School of poetry occupies a place of some importance in the history of Sung poetry. Men of the next era of Sung poetry such as Yang Wan-li and Liu K'o-chuang of the final period of the Southern Sung, occasionally referred to it, and critics of later centuries — among them, the Ch'ing scholar Wang Shih-chen — have made it a subject of study. It was already recognized in Sung times that Ch'en Shih-tao should not be listed among the men of the Chiang-hsi School, and, as I have pointed out, his poetry does not resemble that of the leader of that school, Huang T'ing-chien. There were a number of the other poets of the Chiang-hsi School who were not really success-ful followers of the Huang T'ing-chien style, though they consciously attempted to be. We may point to Lü Chü-jen as an example — the man who drew up the genealogy for the group and who counted himself among the imitators of the Huang style; his poetic works, *Tung-lai hsien-sheng shih-chi*, in twenty *chüan*, have been preserved in the Diet Library in Japan and have recently been reprinted in China. Huang T'ing-chien, as we have seen, had a fondness for the little details of daily life, and observed them closely because he hoped to discover within them some larger meaning. But Lü Chü-jen, in attempting to carry on Huang's style, took over only his taste for detail without any of the deeper significance, and his poetry succeeds in being merely miniature. Again, the so-called "raw words" which Huang and the others of the earlier period had employed to create a kind of antipoetic effect were no longer used by these later poets; indeed, they would have been incapable of knowing how to use them.

Looking back over the period, we see that the great poets of the Northern Sung were able to achieve in their work a narrative and discursive ease — an ease which at times seemed almost inimical to the poetry itself — precisely because they were men of broad character and possessed an intellectual training and discipline to match their moral stature. Ou-yang Hsiu, Wang An-shih, and Su Tung-p'o were all first-rate scholars, and Mei Yao-ch'en and Huang T'ing-chien did not stand far below them. It would be too much to expect that men of such stature would continue to appear in generation after generation. Much less could one hope to find worthy successors to such men among the minor poets of the first half of the twelfth century, a gray age in China's political and literary history.

But if no one could be found to carry on the style of the Northern Sung poets, then poetry must set off in some new direction and it was one of Su Tung-p'o's disciples, Ch'en Shih-tao, as we have seen, who took the first step. In the period that followed him, the outstanding exponent of this new direction was Ch'en Yü-yi.

Ch'en Yü-yi (1090–1138)

In an age of minor poets Ch'en Yü-yi is probably the one whose works most amply repay a reading. Born in the Northern Sung period, he entered government service in 1113 at the age of twenty-four, and continued to serve under Emperor Hui-tsung until the downfall of the Northern Sung. Among the poems written during this period of his life, a series of five in seven-character *chüeh-chü* form called "The Ink-drawn Plums" were said to have won the admiration of Emperor Hui-tsung. Among them the following poem in particular is also mentioned by Chu Hsi in the *Chu-tzu yü-lei*, ch. 140. Ching-lo, as noted earlier, is another name for Pien-ching, the capital of the Northern Sung.

> Lovely, the ten-thousand-jeweled princess of Chiang-nan!
> Since we parted, how many springs have I seen return?
> We meet again in Ching-lo and all is as before,
> But I hate to see the black dust smudge her white robe.
>
> (50:4/4b)

Another seven-character *chüeh-chü* "On the Road to Chung-mou," was written toward the close of the Northern Sung period when the poet was moving about from one to another of a series of posts in the provinces. It describes a stage in the poet's journey as he reaches Chung-mou-hsien, a small city near the capital which he had visited in the past. Crossing the North China plains, the first thing a traveler saw as he approached a city was usually the city wall and the top of the Buddhist pagoda soaring above it.

> It looks as though it wants to rain but rain never falls;
> Returning clouds – see! – they come along with the traveler.
> Same as ever – the crumbling walls of Chung-mou-hsien,
> The thousand-foot pagoda in charge of welcomes and send-offs.
>
> (50:10/1a)

Ch'en Yü-yi was thirty-seven when the Northern Sung fell. Like so many other officials, he fled south to avoid the Chin invaders, and for several years moved about in the provinces of Honan, Hupei, Hunan, Fukien, and Chekiang. Eventually he was invited to take a post in the government of Emperor Kao-tsung at Hangchow, where he became assistant to the prime minister. He died in 1138 at the age of forty-nine. The following seven-character *chüeh-chü* called "Peonies" was written in his late years. The Yi and Lo are two rivers of Honan which run close by the city of Loyang. The Loyang region was the poet's birthplace and was noted for its *mu-tan,* or woody peonies. At the time the poem was written the Loyang area was of course in the hands of the Chin barbarians. Green Mound Creek was in T'ung-hsiang-hsien in Chekiang. "East wind" in Chinese poetry indicates the wind of spring.

> Since barbarian dust first entered the China passes,
> Ten years: the road to the Yi and Lo is long.
> On the bank of Green Mound Creek, a stranger, old and feeble,
> In the east wind stands alone looking at the peonies.
>
> (50:30/4a)

All the examples quoted so far are descriptions of landscapes and are marked by a simple lyricism. Ou-yang Hsiu's narrative tendencies, Su Tung-p'o's boldness, Huang T'ing-chien's obscurity, have all vanished, and we are left with something that is close to the quiet lucidity of T'ang poetry. In form, too, Ch'en Yü-yi's poetry is close to the T'ang; poems in regulated verse and *chüeh-chü* form abound, and there are few longer works in old poetry form.

Ch'en, from his early days, had a fondness for the works of Tu Fu, and this fondness was greatly increased, as he himself tells us, by the fact that in later life he underwent the same experiences of war and flight that Tu Fu had known. In a preface to Ch'en's poems written by someone else, Ch'en is quoted as saying that the poets of his century had learned to respect Tu Fu; but as a result, he added, Su Tung-p'o ended up writing poetry that was "abandoned," and Huang T'ing-chien poetry that was "forced." "One must first recognize what it is that Su and Huang *did not* succeed in imitating before he can cross over to the realm of Master Tu." In other words, in order to appreciate the real greatness of Tu Fu, one must realize how many more worlds he was able to explore than were Su Tung-p'o and Huang T'ing-chien in later centuries. The remark shows that Ch'en was aware that the age of Su Tung-p'o and Huang T'ing-chien had come to an end and that new efforts were needed if one was to continue, like the men of the past, to draw inspiration from Tu Fu.

In Ch'en Yü-yi's case the effort took form in a lyricism based upon a new sensitivity, particularly a sensitivity to the changes of light. Here, for example, is a poem in five-character regulated verse written in 1130, almost five years after the fall of the Northern Sung. It describes the night-darkened hills of Fukien to which the poet had fled.

> Tonight – what night is it?
> I face the dark green of these hills.
> I've stolen life a full five years;
> My secret will is now set firmer.
> Thin shadows encircle all the trees;
> In the still night I hear a single fountain.
> With such solitary things as these alone
> I will live out the years remaining.   (50:24/9b)

The shining of a spider web in the evening sun — this too was the kind of thing that caught Ch'en Yü-yi's eye. Here is another poem in five-character regulated verse entitled "Spring Rain."

> Flowers are gone but spring is still cold;
> The traveler's heart feels only alarm.
> A lone oriole sings through the long noon;
> Fine rain wets the tall battlements.
> Bustle and noise – what do they gain?
> Soft and still I will live out my life.
> Spider threads gleam in the cloudless evening.
> Everywhere I look – the theme of a poem.
>   (50:15/7b)

In another poem we find a similar line: "The spider web glints, now bright, now dark" (50:19/36a).

In the seven-character chüeh-chü, "In Search of Poems," Ch'en establishes a direct connection between the sensation of light and the composition of his poems:

> I love to dip the wild gourd — don't laugh at me;
> Wine has wonderful power, when I'm sad, to bring on sleep.
> Sobering up, I push open the door and go in search of poems.
> Giant trees are tall and craggy in the bright moonlight.
>   (50:21/1a)

The poet's thoughts and feelings, which have been gradually taking shape in the period during and after his drunken sleep, crystallize at last when he opens the door and walks out into the moonlit forest.

Ch'en Yü-yi, even in the midst of his uncertain wanderings, often expressed the optimistic view that life is a process of "multiplication and division" — that is, an alternating rise and fall of fortune and prosperity; and, like a typical Sung man, he attempted to avoid a preoccupation with sorrow alone. "The safety in man's life lies in the multiplications and divisions" (50:22/8b). "With multiplications and divisions I grow old, hoping for a time of peace" (50:23/2b). "With these multiplications and divisions alone I'll bring my life to a close" (50:13/2b).

A lyricism founded upon a sensual perception of nature is of course a quality in which T'ang poetry excels, and an undercurrent of nostalgia for the poetry of the T'ang runs through all the poetry of the Southern Sung period from this time on. Ch'en Yü-yi seems to have tried in his poetry to open up and explore new areas of sensation that had not been explored by the T'ang poets. He himself, however, succeeded merely in creating delicate miniatures; it remained for the superior poets of the succeeding era to bring this new lyricism to its maturity.

Contemporary with Ch'en Yü-yi were the poets Tseng Chi, the teacher of the famous poet Lu Yu; Liu Tzu-hui, teacher of the philosopher Chu Hsi; and Chu Hsi's father, Chu Sung. All wrote poetry which is close in feeling to that of Ch'en Yü-yi. In addition, Chu Sung has left us his critical remarks on poetry, in which he expresses the opinion that, although many of the T'ang poets deserve to be criticized on grounds of moral character, still, "from the time when poets first existed, there have never been any more glorious than those of the T'ang." "When Li Po and Tu Fu of the T'ang appeared, all other poets of past and present faded from sight" (56:9/8a–11a), he declares, expressing the nostalgia for T'ang poetry that was becoming increasingly acute at this time.

I will close this section with a poem by Tseng Chi (1084–1166), the teacher of Lu Yu, who will be the subject of the section that follows. It is a five-character old poem called "Dozing on My Mat." The mat of the title was a round one made of rushes and used as a sitting cushion.

A man of retirement sits in the clear autumn,
Weary from staring at the words of ancient sages.
After a thousand breaths that reach to the groin,
My spirit suddenly goes blank and still.
Little did I expect the dark sweet land of sleep,
Yet in this I've discovered the shortest road there.
Sprawling in bed isn't always best;
I've chanced upon a better way.
Waking up, I yawn and stretch,
My eyes still open only half way.
My body doesn't know where it is;
My mind is a long time getting focused.
From now on, goodby to quilt and bed curtain;
A rush mat will do for my daily nap.   (2:1/10)

Chapter Six

THE MIDDLE YEARS OF THE

SOUTHERN SUNG

1150–1200

Lu Yu (1125–1209)

Sung poetry reached its second peak of excellence in the latter part of the twelfth century and the beginning of the thirteenth. Emperor Hsiao-tsung, the adopted son to whom Emperor Kao-tsung, the first ruler of the Southern Sung, had ceded his throne in 1163, bestowed on his predecessor the honorary title of Grand Supreme Emperor, and reigned until 1189. He took a more aggressive attitude toward the Chin invaders than his predecessor, and dispatched armies in an attempt to regain control of the north. But the attempt failed, and he was obliged to conclude another treaty of peace with the Chin, the so-called "Peace of the *Lung-hsing* Era." The names of Su Tung-p'o and the others of his political group had gradually come back into good repute from the beginning of the Southern Sung period, and Emperor Hsiao-tsung, as one of his acts of state, bestowed upon Su Tung-p'o the posthumous title "Wen-chung Kung," or Cultured and Loyal Duke. After occupying the throne for twenty-eight years, Emperor Hsiao-tsung followed the example of his predecessor by ceding the throne to his son, who became Emperor Kuang-tsung. But Emperor Kuang-tsung was sickly and in 1194 was obliged to cede the throne to his son, who became Emperor Ning-tsung. Emperor Ning-tsung reigned for thirty years, from 1194 until 1224, and it was during these years that Sung poetry attained its second flowering.

Lu Yu (1125–1209) was the greatest poet of this period, but his name is often linked with that of the other two outstanding poets of the time, Fan Ch'eng-ta (1126–1193) and Yang Wan-li (1124–1206). As may be seen from their dates, the three men were born in consecutive years — the last three years of the Northern Sung — and all were friends. All three grew up during the reign of Emperor Kao-tsung, but only Fan Ch'eng-ta has left us the poems of his youthful period. Both Lu Yu and Yang Wan-li destroyed their early works, perhaps as a gesture of silent protest against the weak-kneed attitude which Emperor Kao-tsung took toward the Chin invaders.

Lu Yu lived to be eighty-five, and the poems written during the fifty-odd years from the age of thirty-two until his death have all been collected in the 85-*chüan* work entitled *Chien-nan shih-kao*, which contains nearly ten thousand poems. They are arranged chronologically according to the dates the poet himself assigned to them. The size of his output increased with age. Between the ages of forty-six and fifty-four, when he was an official in the border region of Szechwan, he was a prolific writer, and during the last twenty years of his life, when he lived in retirement in a farming village near Shao-hsing, his old home, in Chekiang, he composed almost at the rate of a poem a day. Such productivity, though not unmatched in later centuries, certainly had no precedent in the earlier history of Chinese literature. The volume of his work alone is enough to stagger one, and to impress upon one the fact that he was a man of great activity. And a look at these ten thousand poems will show that very few of them are either slipshod or perfunctory. Every poem seems to be a finished work. A spirit of action informs each one and brings it to fulfillment as a poem, whether the scale is large or small.

Lu Yu was by nature a man of action. His political views centered about the conviction that China should launch an all-out attack on its enemy, the Chin. From time to time in his poetry he expressed the wish that he could join the army, march into enemy territory, and help to "wrap the dead in their shrouds of horse hide." Again and again we find references to his longing for the day of attack, as in the following couplet:

> Shame, that the history books of the ages won't bear my name!
> All of this pure red heart I give to the Son of Heaven.

(4:4/11b)

Or this one, which envisions an attack on the north:

> If one morning you crossed the border – try it and see!
> At dawn you'd leave Pao-chi, by evening you're in Ch'ang-an!
>
> (4:9/1a)

And in the poem entitled "To Show to My Sons" which he wrote on his deathbed, he concluded with these words:

> The day the royal armies march north and seize the central plain,
> Don't forget to sacrifice and report it to your father!   (4:85/6b)

This love of action, revealed both in his attitude toward poetic composition and in his political views, stemmed from the fact that he was a passionate man, and his passions were intensified by the frustrations he suffered. First of all, his call for an invasion of the north was from time to time forcibly silenced by the government authorities. The Ch'ing critic Chao Yi has pointed out that one of the peculiarities of Lu Yu's works is the large number of poems that deal with dreams; but this is hardly surprising when we think that it was in dreams alone that an attack upon the Chin became a possibility. In the prefatory remarks to a poem in seven-character old form written in 1180, when he was fifty-six, the poet writes: "On the eleventh day of the fifth month, just before midnight, I dreamt I was accompanying the carriage of the Son of Heaven, who had gone in person to attack and recover possession of all the old Han and T'ang territories . . . As I was riding along on my horse, I began composing a long poem, but before I could finish it I woke up" (4:12/8a-b). In common with the other men of the Southern Sung, he had little knowledge of the real situation in the north under the Chin rulers. For example, in a poem written in 1184, he declared: "The chief of the barbarians has returned north of the Gobi Desert" (4:16/10a); and "The rule of the barbarians has fallen into decay and chaos!" (4:16/14a), urging that the moment for an attack had come. As a matter of fact, however, the Chin state at this time, headed by the wise and capable Emperor Shih-tsung, was enjoying its period of greatest peace and stability. This ignorance of the true situation beyond the borders served to increase the poet's sense of frustration.

Frustration marred his family life as well. By his mother's order he was forced to divorce his first wife, an experience which he recalled with bitterness in a poem written when he was sixty-three. In seven-character old form and entitled "The Chrysanthemum Pillow," it recalls an earlier pillow stuffed with chrysanthemum petals that his first wife had made for him long ago.

> I pick yellow flowers to stuff a pillow with;
> The folded screen, the deep curtains, hold in the rich scent,
> Calling back a dream of forty-three years ago.
> The lamp is dark, there's no one to tell my heartache to.
>
> (4:19/6a)

In his young married days he had written a poem on the earlier chrysanthemum pillow, as he tells us in the following poem, though the earlier verse has not survived.

> When I was young, I made a poem on the chrysanthemum pillow –
> Wormy volumes, bits of manuscript lie wrapped in cobwebs.
> All things of mankind fade and wear away;
> Only the clear fragrance remains as it was before.   (4:19/6a)

The upsurge of frustrated passion led in Lu Yu's case to the composition of many poems of feeling, and for this reason his poetry gives a quite different impression from that of the earlier years of the Sung, particularly of the Northern Sung period. There is no longer any denial of sorrow, and feeling is frankly revealed. Indeed, feeling is the quality which colors the vast sea of his poetry. Dipping into this great sea for a few examples, we may cite the following poem written in 1177, when the poet was fifty-three and held a post in Szechwan. It is in seven-character regulated verse and is called "Autumn Thoughts." The sound of mallets pounding the cloth for uniforms reminds him of the frustrating and slipshod nature of his own life and of the military and political situation.

> In the west wind, fulling mallets busily pound uniforms;
> Now is the time for the traveler to take note.
> From the first all was meant merely to be like this!
> Over half my hundred years are gone – where shall I go from here?
> The cricket in the painted hall complains to the clear night;

By the iron-curbed well, pagoda tree leaves fall from old limbs.
A pillow of sharp loneliness will not let me sleep.
I call for a lamp and get up to write a poem on autumn thoughts.

(4:8/13b)

The following poem, also in seven-character regulated verse and named "Sorrowing over Autumn," was written in 1184 when the poet was at his old home in Shao-hsing in Chekiang. The lake mentioned is that known as Mirror Lake, beside which the poet's house stood.

After illness, all out of kilter, I can't hold myself upright.
The lakeside is sad and lonely, the cold comes early.
I've already wondered at these white hairs, an aging Feng T'ang;
Now the clear autumn rouses the sorrow of Sung Yü.
Above my pillow, many voices — wild geese newly come;
In front of the lamp, a chessboard, the pieces still in place.
A man has certain things he feels in his heart,
But Heaven and Earth are feelingless and seem not to know.

(4:16/14b)

Feng T'ang was an official of the second century B.C. who served at the Han court but, at odds with the times, he lived to the age of ninety without advancing to a high post. Sung Yü, a poet of the state of Ch'u who flourished around 275 B.C., is the author of the *Chiu-pien*, or "Nine Arguments," a cycle of poems lamenting the sadness of autumn.[1] The last line of the poem may be interpreted in various ways. Here I will only point out that it bears a close resemblance to a line in a poem I shall quote a little later which reads: "Useless to call to Heaven — how can it hear?"

Lu Yu seems to have reacted against the almost excessive coolness and lack of passion that appear from time to time in the poetry of the Northern Sung. Signs of such a reaction are already to be found among Lu Yu's predecessors in the early years of the Southern Sung. It was a reaction which affected the whole poetic world of the day, and led, it would seem, to the nostalgic attitude toward T'ang poetry which I have already mentioned. But although the tendency toward reaction existed

---

[1] See David Hawkes, *Ch'u Tz'u — The Songs of the South, An Ancient Chinese Anthology* (Oxford, 1959), pp. 92ff [Tr.].

before him, it was Lu Yu who, through his passionate and active personality, actually succeeded in bringing lyricism to life again.

Lu Yu himself believed that his poetry was closest to that of Tu Fu, particularly in the quality of passion. He seems to have had great respect for Tu Fu's work even from his early days, and from around the age of fifty, when he became an official in Szechwan, the region where Tu Fu had spent the latter part of his life, his interest in and sympathy for Tu Fu's poetry increased in intensity. The fact that about half of his ten thousand poems are in Tu Fu's favorite poetic form, seven-character regulated verse, may be said to reflect Tu Fu's influence. Moreover, the way in which, in these seven-character regulated verse poems such as "Autumn Thoughts" quoted above, he uses creatures and objects from the natural world — in this instance the cricket and the pagoda tree — to heighten the emotional intensity of the poem, is in keeping with the practice of Tu Fu and of T'ang poetry generally. But whereas in T'ang poetry we usually find both lines of a couplet being used to describe some natural scene or object, Lu Yu more often devotes half of the couplet to nature and half to man, as in his "Sorrowing over Autumn":

> Above my pillow, many voices – wild geese newly come;
> In front of the lamp, a chessboard, the pieces still in place.

The difference is probably attributable to the exalted view of man's importance that prevailed in Sung thought and poetry. A careful analysis of Lu Yu's numerous poems in seven-character regulated verse might well reveal a number of interesting facts about his technique.

But Lu Yu's passionate feelings did not always find expression in the same way as those of Tu Fu. They did not, for example, lead him into the headlong burst of lamentation that was common with Tu Fu, in which both the world and the poet himself were forgotten. Lu Yu was, after all, a man of the Sung and, whether he was aware of it or not, an heir of the broad-visioned philosophy, the philosophy of resistance, which had come down to him from Su Tung-p'o. Perhaps as a form of reaction against Northern Sung poetry, he did not, like Su Tung-p'o, expound his philosophy in his poems. Yet the ten thousand poems in his collected works are by no means barren of statements indicating what his philosophy was.

First of all, like Su Tung-p'o, he recognized that sorrow and grief are ubiquitous and constitute an essential element of human life. Other poems might be cited to illustrate the point, but here let me quote a poem in seven-character old form written in 1176 and entitled "Spring Sadness."

> Spring sadness, vast and wide, blankets earth and sky.
> Before I reach where I'm going, sadness gets there first,
> Filling the eyes like clouds suddenly blowing up,
> Visiting men like a fever – how can they escape?
> A guest comes, urging me to pass the cups and tallies;
> I laugh and tell him, let it be!
> The drunkard will fall down, the sad man will be sad.
> Sadness and wine can do nothing for each other.   (4:8/2b)

The "tallies" mentioned in line five were used when guests were drinking to keep track of how many cups of wine each guest had had; thus no guest could refuse the host's invitation to another cup on the excuse that he had already had too many.

In the poem "Spring Sadness" we see the recognition of sorrow as a frequent and inescapable element of human life, a view often expressed in Lu Yu's works. The best example from his late years is probably the set of five poems in seven-character *chüeh-chü* form written when the poet was eighty-four, which bear the heading, "Written as a joke after reading some of the T'ang poets' poems on sadness." The following is the first of the series.

> When I was young I asked, what kind of thing is sorrow?
> Now I'm old I understand that the world is sorrowful,
> And though we forget the world, sorrow will still be there.
> Only if we could forget ourselves would it ever go away.
>
> (4:80/2a)

Having recognized the inescapability of sorrow, he goes on in the second poem of the series to relate the existence of sorrow to poetry.

Pure sadness is what we make our poems of;
Without sadness, how would we have any poems?
Be it that of a lonely night spent by the temple window,
Or that when one journeys past the post lodge in the mountains.

(4:80/2a)

But Lu Yu followed Su Tung-p'o in his view that sorrow is not the only element in life, and that happiness too is to be found throughout life. As an example, we may note the following poem written in 1174 when the poet was on his way to Szechwan. Along the way he stopped briefly in the library of a younger scholar named Huang; the poem, in five-character old form and called "Resting in the Library of Huang *Hsiu-ts'ai*," records the experience. Not only does the poet's philosophy resemble that of Su Tung-p'o; the opening simile recalls Su's line: "My life is made of sojourns only."

My life is like an empty boat
Drifting forever ten thousand miles.
Hating to end my days a wanderer,
Everywhere I go I think of tying up.
By the side of the road, who lives here?
Flowers and bamboo are so still and calm.
The gate, the garden, are clean as though polished;
The windows, the desk, are bright mirrors to look into.
The room has shelves piled high with books,
Carefully collated with notes in red ink.
It I could bring some thatch and build next door,
Though I grew old, who would I have to envy?   (4:5/15a)

Again he is like Su Tung-p'o in his belief that life, which is like "an empty boat" drifting on the water, is to be lived in a spirit of resistance. Perhaps the clearest expression of this idea is to be found in the following poem, "The Stone on the Hilltop," written in 1193 when the poet was sixty-nine. It is in old form with a mixture of five-character and seven-character lines. The "old man" of the poem is the poet himself.

Autumn wind: ten thousand trees wither;
Spring rain: a hundred grasses grow.
Is this really some plan of the Creator,

This flowering and fading, each season that comes?
Only the stone there on the hilltop,
Its months and years too many to count,
Knows nothing of the four-season round,
Wearing its constant colors unchanged.
The old man has lived all his life in these hills;
Though his legs fail him, he still clambers up,
Now and then strokes the rock and sighs three sighs:
How can I make myself stony like you?   (4:28/3b)

The view of cyclical change expressed in the opening lines of the poem leads the poet to search for some being that resists change. He finds it in the stone on the hilltop, which he climbs up the hill to stroke and admire, wondering if he too can acquire the power to resist change. The poet seems to have adopted this philosophy of resistance fairly early in life; we find it already in the poem entitled "White Hair" written in Szechwan at the age of fifty, where, in the lines,

My life is truly full of turnings;
Nine detours on the road to old age,   (4:6/13a)

the words recall Su Tung-p'o's lines in the poem already quoted.

I've had a lot of trouble from the time I was young,
Dodging and threading my way through life.

Lu Yu's poetry, while rich in sentiment, is not wholly given up to it, because he embraced and carried on the broad-visioned philosophy which he had inherited from Su Tung-p'o. His upbringing also was such as to encourage this breadth of vision. From the time of his grandfather Lu Tien, his family had been scholars; among other studies, they specialized in medicine and herb lore, which resulted in Lu Yu often doling out medicines to the farmers in the regions where he lived. Needless to say, this was not his only study. In a poem called "Reading," written in 1177, he tells how he spent his evenings at that time. In a note which he himself added he explains that he was reading an edition of Ssu-ma Kuang's voluminous history, the *Tzu-chih t'ung-chien* or *General Mirror for the Aid of Government*, which was printed in the tiny characters known as *ying-t'ou* or "fly's head." The poem is in seven-character old form:

> If I want to retire, don't I have my five-acre farm?
> The reason I go on reading is for the sake of the people.
> Though the strength of my eyes by lamplight isn't what it used to be,
> I can still get through twenty thousand fly's head characters a night.
>
> (4:8/4a)

Lu Yu believed that it was his responsibility as an official to continue to read and study so that he could serve the people more efficiently, a fact which indicates the breadth of his viewpoint.

The passionate nature he was born with and the breadth of vision he acquired through his studies combined in Lu Yu's poetry to produce a third quality — one which was probably more important than either of these. He was a man of passion, but he did not allow this to constrict his field of vision. And when passion is given play in an unrestricted field of vision, the result will be a multisided perception of reality. This is the third quality of Lu's poetry. But he did not seek to resolve this many-sided vision of reality in terms of abstract philosophy. For him, the apprehension of reality through sensation was the most fitting approach for a man of active mind. During his later years, when the reality about him was the life of the countryside, his observation was especially keen and active. China has had many pastoral poets from the time of T'ao Yüan-ming on, but none has succeeded as well as Lu Yu in capturing the variety and color of farm life.

Let me merely list here the contents of some of these poems on life in the countryside. Though my list is by no means a complete one, I note that there are first of all poems dealing with the farmers' tasks during the four seasons, as well as on the celebrations accompanying New Years, the Dragon Boat Festival, and times of abundant harvest. Next are poems dealing with marriage, tax-paying, and tax dodgers (*Chien-nan shih-kao*, ch. 59); the village doctor (ch. 59); the village dispensers of medicine, among whom Lu Yu himself is included (ch. 72); the dentist who makes false teeth (ch. 56); the tailor (ch. 39); the hat-maker (ch. 39); the old man who sells firewood (ch. 69); the wineshop keeper who annoys people by pounding a drum in the evening to attract customers (ch. 64); the Buddhist priest (ch. 40); the physiognomist (ch. 29); the diviner (ch. 32); the theatrical performers and storytellers (ch. 27, 32, 33, 53, 68, 80); the old actor (ch. 26); the iron plaque which is pounded at five o'clock in the morning to indicate that it is time to begin work in the field (ch. 20); the communal meals of the farmers (ch. 45); the hired hands called "guests" employed during the busy season (ch. 66); road repairing (ch. 45); the village school, which begins in the tenth month and in which the children use, as a textbook in learning characters, a work called *Pai-chia-hsing* or *The Hundred Family Names* (ch. 22, 25); the tea house (ch. 77); the dovecote (ch. 61); the bridegroom who gets drafted the day after his wedding (ch. 69); the quarrels of the villagers (ch. 62, 70); the thief (ch. 24, 60); and other topics. In other words, in Lu Yu's poems the life of a farming village in eastern Chekiang in the twelfth and thirteenth centuries is reflected in the minutest detail.

The descriptions in these poems are made even more vivid by the sympathy and respect which the poet himself feels for the labors of the farmers. Here, for example, is one of a series of poems in five-character regulated verse entitled "Farm Families," written just before his death, when he was eighty-four:

> Snug — the robe sewn from coarse cotton;
> Red — the fire kindled from dry sticks.
> Meager talents I give to the countryside;
> Simple learning I teach the young boys:
> For sheep you want a pen that's high,
> For chickens, a closely-woven basket.
> Farm families have joys of their own,
> Not in a class with those of kings. (4:78/7b)

Or the following, the sixth poem in the same series, which describes the farm children returning from the village school.

> It's late, the children come home from school;
> Braids unplaited, they ramble the fields,
> Jeering at each other — guess what's in my hand!
> Arguing — who won the grass fight after all?

Father sternly calls them to lessons;
Grandfather indulgently feeds them candy.
We don't ask you to become rich and famous,
But when the time comes, work hard in the fields!

(4:78/8a)

Lu Yu's feeling for the farm people was deepened by the fact that in his old age he lived on a meager government pension and did some farming himself, so that he consciously identified himself with the farmers. The following pieces give a glimpse of the poet at work on his farm. The first, in seven-character regulated verse, is the first of four poems called "Little Garden." The poet is reading the poems of T'ao Yüan-ming.

Mist-veiled plants in the little garden reach to the house next door;
Mulberry trees make deep shade, one small path slanting through.
I lie down to read T'ao's poems – less than one chapter,
When fine rain brings an excuse to jump up and hoe the melons.

(4:13/6b)

The second, in five-character old form, is entitled "The Farm House in Late Fall."

I'm getting close on seventy,
The world forgotten long ago.
Luckily my strength hasn't left me;
A bit unsteady, I can still tend the farm.
Living here among these other old farmers,
How can I hide from wind and frost?
At midnight when I get up to feed the oxen
The Big Dipper hangs on the far horizon.   (4:23/5a)

Life was not always easy for Lu Yu, as we see in the following poem in seven-character old form. Written when he was seventy-one, it bears this heading: "Being so poor, I wrote this short song to air my worries."

The year is rich, rice is cheap – I alone am hungry.
This morning I got some rice, but no wood for cooking.
Earth is eighty thousand li from Heaven –
Useless to call to Heaven – how can it hear?   (4:33/10a)

Lu Yu had six sons, for whom he felt great affection. Because he lived so long, he saw them all grow up and go off to other parts of the country to seek employment. His poems addressed to them are filled with tenderness, as may be seen in the long poem written in 1202 when the poet's second son, Tzu-lung, set off for Chi-chou in Kiangsi to take an official post. These poems are particularly interesting because the theme of a father's love for his sons is rare in Chinese poetry.

Lu Yu's familial affection extended even to his cats. He has left us poems describing one cat named "Snow Child" (ch. 23), and another named "Powder Nose" (ch. 28), but here I shall quote a third example, a seven-character *chüeh-chü* entitled simply "To Give to the Cat."

> I wrapped up salt and took it in exchange for the little cat
> Who guards all the numberless books in my study.
> I'm ashamed to be so poor, to feed him so skimpily –
> No carpet for the cold, no supper of fish.   (4:42/11a)

The custom of taking a gift of salt in exchange for a cat is mentioned in another poem in *chüan* 42. A seven-character old poem written when the poet was in Szechwan gives us another glimpse of his family life. Reading like a passage from an autobiographical novel, it describes how his youngest son came to his study in the evening to ask his father to correct a poem he had written, and how the boy soon became drowsy and went off to bed, leaving the poet facing the cat that sits on the rug (*chüan* 18).

But the most intense affection he felt was for his country and countrymen, a fact which has led recent literary historians to dub him "The Patriot-Poet." His patriotism centered about the call for an attack upon the hated Chin, but he longed for war solely because he believed that in the end it would bring benefit to his fellow countrymen. Like Wang An-shih, he also advocated a more equal distribution of land, as may be seen in a poem written in 1194, "Thoughts on Old Age." In another (*chüan* 76) he writes that "farming and sericulture are the basis of good government," a conviction which, he tells us, he held from the time when, as a child, he studied the "Airs of Pin" section of the *Book of Odes*, which deals with the yearly round of farm tasks.

The following poem in seven-character regulated verse, written when the poet was eighty-four, gives clear expression to the strong sense of social responsibility that underlies all his poetry. It bears the following heading: "There are many who cannot get through the winter nights in the village; in grief I wrote this poem."

> In the time of old age, sickness day by day invades me;
> Long ago I gave up my meager pay to lie down in hilly woods.
> Though I do not say how I pity the aged and lament the humble,
> My mind grieves at poverty, sorrows for those oppressed.
> My purse is too empty to offer a single meal,
> Though duty makes me wish I could scatter boundless gold.
> Night deepens as my fervor stirs by the fading lamp;
> These shining solitary thoughts God will look down on.
>
> (4:79/4b)

And in the seven-character *chüeh-chü* called "Sitting up at Night" and written the same year, we once more see the octogenarian poet sitting with his "solitary thoughts," longing to be of some use to the world.

> Spinners' lights from house to house brighten the deep night;
> Here and there new fields have been plowed after rain.
> Always I feel ashamed to be so old and idle.
> Sitting close by the stove, I hear the sound of wind.   (4:79/7b)

The following year, after bidding farewell to the world in a poem entitled "To Show to My Sons," he died at the age of eighty-five.

One of the earliest appraisals of Lu Yu's poetry is that found in a poem by Tai Fu-ku [2] in seven-character regulated verse called "Reading the *Chien-nan shih-kao* by Mr. Fang-weng." He writes of Lu Yu that "During the hundred years since the move south [that is, since the Sung court moved to Hangchow], there has been no one to equal him." He then goes on to praise the simplicity of Lu Yu's themes and diction:

> Using what is plain and simple he fashioned subtle lines;
> Taking the most ordinary words, he changed them into wonders.
>
> (39:6/20a)

He also notes the extreme breadth of Lu Yu's subject matter, stating

---

[2] See Chapter Seven.

that of all the themes treated by Li Po, Tu Fu, Ch'en Shih-tao, and Huang T'ing-chien, Lu Yu "tried his hand at them all and left none untouched."

Fan Ch'eng-ta (1126–1193)

Fan Ch'eng-ta was born in 1126, a year after Lu Yu. He served as governor of Szechwan, where Lu Yu was one of his subordinates, and eventually rose to the highest position in the government, that of *Ts'an-chih cheng-shih*, or prime minister. In keeping with a position of such importance he has left us a collection of poems in thirty-three *chüan* entitled *Shih-hu chü-chih shih-chi*, containing 1916 poems. Less varied and less bold than those of Lu Yu, they are at the same time more refined and orthodox in nature. The rough, almost uncouth, impression one sometimes gets from Lu Yu's poetry is entirely absent. Lu Yu was a native of Shao-hsing, east of the Ch'ien-t'ang River in Chekiang, while Fan Ch'eng-ta came from Suchow in Kiangsu. In the later history of literature and art the differences between the men of the Che, or Chekiang, group, and those of the Wu, or Kiangsu, group, were to be of great importance, and it is possible that these differences had already begun to take shape in the time of Lu Yu and Fan Ch'eng-ta.

Fan Ch'eng-ta spent much time moving about from one provincial post to another, and we find a number of travel poems among his works. The following, in seven-character regulated verse, is entitled "On the Road to Kao-ch'un." Kao-ch'un was near Nanking in Kiangsu and was probably a rich farming region.

My way enters Kao-ch'un; wheat grows deeper still;
Mud splatters wet on the grass as the horse races by.
Rains settle on the head of the field, clouds congeal to form eye-shadow;
Sunlight leaks from the waist of the hill, stones ooze gold.
Though it isn't spring, the flowers of the old willow hang in coils;
The ancient shrine is wall-less, trees shade it in vain.
The lunch box will be for the teahouse in the coming village.
Cooking smoke rises thick from the bamboo grove.   (38:5/2b)

A rather special kind of trip was that which Fan took in 1170 as

envoy to the enemy state of Chin in the north. He has left us a poetic
record of this journey in a series of seven-character *chüeh-chü*. When
he was passing through the old Sung capital, Pien-ching (K'ai-feng)
he stopped at the Hsiang-kuo-ssu, in former days one of the liveliest
and most prosperous Buddhist temples of the city. It was festival day
at the temple, but all he saw displayed in the open-air stalls within the
temple grounds were the goods of the Jurchen Tartars. The "imperial
plaque" hanging below the eaves was that written by Emperor Hui-
tsung and presented to the temple in the late years of the Northern
Sung.

> Tilting eaves, their edges broken, guard the imperial plaque;
> The gold and jade-green pagoda is grimed with old dust.
> They say this morning I'm in luck – the temple is open;
> Sheep's fur robes, wolf skin caps are all the fashion now.
>
> (38:12/3a)

The poem should be read in conjunction with Fan's prose account of
the journey found in his *Lan-p'ei-lu*, or *Record of Holding the Carriage
Reins*. He is in fact famous for his travelogues; that entitled *Wu-ch'uan-
lu*, or *Record of the Ship of Wu*, describing the journey down the
Yangtze from Szechwan which he took in 1177, is often mentioned
along with the similar work by Lu Yu, the *Ju-shu-chi*, or *Account of a
Journey to Szechwan*.

Among Fan Ch'eng-ta's works the most familiar to Japanese readers
is the series of sixty poems (each a seven-character *chüeh-chü*) called
"Ssu-shih t'ien-yüan tsa-hsing," or "Farm Scenes of the Four Seasons."
Written in 1186 when the poet was sixty-one, they describe the year-
round scenes of farm life at his country estate outside Suchow. Here
is the first of the series, a scene in spring.

> Willow flowers, deep lanes, a sound of noonday chickens;
> Mulberry leaves sharp and new, not yet green:
> I doze where I sit, and wake with nothing to do.
> Clear sunlight fills the window – I watch the silkworms grow.
>
> (38:27/1a)

The poems are arranged in five groups of twelve each, entitled
"Spring Days," "Late Spring," "Summer Days," "Fall Days," and

"Winter Days." They were enthusiastically read during the Edo period in Japan, and in feeling are often quite close to the haiku of Buson. Here is one from the group on "Late Spring."

> After a night of rain, the farmhouse is late getting up.
> Dormer windows show new color, half-filled with faint warmth.
> The old man propped on his pillow listens to orioles warbling.
> The boys open the gate so the swallows can fly out.
>
> (38:27/3a)

Similar in theme are the poems dealing with the Shang-yüan, or Fifteenth of the First Month celebration ("Thirty-two Rhymes in Comic Style Recording the Festivals of the Wu Region" [38:23/3b]) and the La-yüeh, or Twelfth Month Festival ("Village Yüeh-fu, Ten Poems" [38:30/1a]), which are interesting for the light they shed upon local customs in the Suchow area. Perhaps because of his high official position, Fan Ch'eng-ta's attitude toward the life of the farmers is more detached than that of Lu Yu and lacking in Lu Yu's warmth.

Yang Wan-li (1127–1206), Chu Hsi (1130–1200), and Others

The third important poet of this period was Yang Wan-li, a man of Kiangsi who was born in 1127. In reference to his poetic works his friend Lou Yüeh, in a poem written for him, remarks:

> Each post you hold results in a collection of poems;
> The number handed down must be close to a thousand chüan.
>
> (28:2/16b)

Lou Yüeh is referring to the fact that each time Yang Wan-li moved to another position in the capital or the provincial government he produced a collection of poems. In the preface to his first collection, entitled Chiang-hu-chi, or River and Lake Collection, Yang reports that at first he wrote poems in the Chiang-hsi style — that is, the style of Huang T'ing-chien — but later burned all these early works. The poems included in his first collection all date from 1162, the year when Emperor Hsiao-tsung came to the throne and Yang Wan-li himself was thirty-six. The poems written when he was studying the five-character regulated verse of Ch'en Shih-tao came first; then those composed while he was studying the seven-character *chüeh-chü* of Wang An-shih; and finally those written when he was studying the seven-character *chüeh-chü* of the T'ang period. His second collection of poems, entitled *Ching-ch'i-chi*, or *Ching-ch'i Collection*, dates from the time when he was governor of Ch'ang-chou in Kiangsu. The preface states that at the time of the New Year's vacation in 1178, at the age of fifty-two, he suddenly experienced a literary awakening. He proceeded to discard all his previous models for poetry, claiming that "the ten thousand phenomena all came to me, offering me their themes for a poem." In his preface to the fifth collection, the *Ch'ao-t'ien shih-chi* (*Returning to the Court*), he remarks in a similar vein: "Whether abroad or at home, sleeping or eating, I have nothing to do with anything but poetry." The preface to his seventh collection, the *Ch'ao-t'ien hsü-chi* (*Returning Again to Court*), dated 1190, when he was sixty-four, reports that the number of poems already published has reached close to three thousand, and two more collections, the *Chiang-tung-chi* (*East of the River*), and the *T'ui-hsiu-chi* (*In Retirement*), appeared before his death in 1206 at the age of eighty. Next to Lu Yu he was the most prolific of the Sung poets.

That Yang Wan-li burned all the poems of his early years, when he had written in the manner of Huang T'ing-chien, indicates that he was not content to follow the models of the Northern Sung period. Moreover, he tried consciously to capture the spirit of T'ang poetry, his predilection for which was even more marked than that of his contemporaries Lu Yu and Fan Ch'eng-ta. The following seven-character *chüeh-chü* was written in the spring of 1178, the year of his poetic awakening, and is called "Reading the Verse of the T'ang Poets and Pan-shan." Pan-shan refers to Wang An-shih.

> Alas, the men of T'ang and Pan-shan tried
> All at once, fiercely, to divide the realm of poetry between them.
> But though Pan-shan could go a long way,
> The T'ang men were still a gateway beyond.   (3:8/13b)

Again, in speaking about what he had learned from the poetry of

Ch'en Shih-tao in a poem in his fourth collection, the *Nan-hai-chi*, or *South Sea Collection*, he says of Ch'en, "He broke through the layer of frost to where the mountain bones are cold." But in another poem, he says, "What is needed is for us to cross the highest gateway of the men of T'ang" (3:16/18b). In writing about the collection of poems entitled *Li-tse ts'ung-shu* by the late T'ang poet Lu Kuei-meng, for which he expressed admiration, he remarked,

> Who can I find to appreciate with me the special flavor of late T'ang?
> Poets nowadays look on the T'ang with scorn.   (3:27/1b)

Emperor Hsiao-tsung, who reigned at this time, was fond of inscribing T'ang period *chüeh-chü* on fans, and with this fact in mind, Hung Mai, a friend of Yang Wan-li, compiled an anthology entitled *T'ang-jen wan-shou chüeh-chü*, or *Ten Thousand Quatrains by T'ang Poets*. It is clear that the fondness for T'ang poetry, particularly that in *chüeh-chü* form, was becoming a fairly common taste at this time.

Yang Wan-li's poetry, however, is by no means a mere imitation of the T'ang style. On the contrary, the value of his work lies mainly in its free and vigorous originality. This may be seen in the poems written even before his "enlightenment." As examples I will quote two seven-character *chüeh-chü* from his first collection of poems, the *Chiang-hu-chi*. The first is one of four poems entitled "Crossing by the Pai-chia Ferry."

> One minute clear, one minute rain – the road dries and gets wet;
> Half dark-hued, half pale, the mountains fold and pile up.
> Amid the level of distant grass I see an ox's back,
> And where new seedlings are far apart, the footprints of a man.
>   (3:1/9b)

The second, in the same form, is called "Feelings in Autumn."

> Times past I never grieved at autumn, but loved it only:
> Flutes sounding in the wind, towers in the moonlight.
> This year autumn's colors are all as they've been before,
> But though I don't want to grieve, I have no way to stop.
>   (3:6/18a)

Yang Wan-li did not by any means confine himself to the *chüeh-chü* form. He had a marked fondness for the older poetic forms with their greater freedom, as may be seen from the following example, one of five "old poems" in five-character lines entitled (like the *chüeh-chü* above) "Feelings in Autumn." It is taken from his sixth collection of poetry, the *Chiang-hsi tao-yüan chi*, or *Chiang-hsi Taoist Temple Collection*.

> All my life I've dreaded long summers;
> Clear autumn — that was what I longed for most.
> Why then, now that fall is here,
> Do I feel no delight, but sorrow instead?
> Books and papers in autumn can be read,
> Verses and couplets in autumn thought out.
> Long nights are good for heavy drinking;
> Broad fields are good for rambling trips.
> Ten thousand hills and streams south of the river
> In one evening will fill these narrow eyes.
> Fetch me my hiking gaiters!
> Where could I go and not find a hill? (3:25/2b)

Yang Wan-li was very free in his diction, making greater use of colloquialisms than any other Sung poet. The scenes he depicts and his manner of expression are also at times striking in their novelty. Here, for example, is a seven-character *chüeh-chü* from his first collection. Entitled "Passing the Bridge Teahouse at Shen-chu," it describes a stop at a teahouse built out over a river and the poet's astonishment when he glanced up and saw the mast of a ship sticking up above the bamboo of the garden.

> I stepped down from the palanquin and stared at the country teahouse,
> Puzzling at the sound of water cold beneath my feet.
> I didn't know beyond the bamboo the long river was so close,
> Till all at once the tip of a tall mast came poking up. (3:5/16b)

This freedom of diction and subject matter has led some critics to regard Yang Wan-li mistakenly as a frivolous writer, though in fact he was a serious scholar, as indicated by his literary name Ch'eng-chai — "Studio of Sincerity" — and the fact that he wrote a commentary on the *Book of Changes* which he called the *Ch'eng-chai yi-chuan*. The more serious side of his nature is well expressed in the following poem, also from his first collection. A seven-character *chüeh-chü*, it bears the heading, "Traveling through Fen-yi, I met a man who came from the same district as I." To the poet, all men, even the most casual acquaintances, are his brothers.

> Sons and daughters left at home weigh lighter on my mind
> When all men I meet along the road are brothers.
> Don't ask if ever we'll think of each other again –
> As time comes to say goodby, I can't help feeling moved.
>
> (3:4/3a)

Yang rose to a much higher official position than Lu Yu, and yet, like Lu Yu, he retained a strong love and sympathy for the common people. In the following poem from his eighth collection, a seven-character *chüeh-chü* entitled "Teahouses by the Road," he points out the feeling for beauty that is apparent even in the lives of the country teahouse keepers.

> Along the road are two or three country teahouses;
> In the clear dawn they've no hot water, much less tea!
> Do you say this shows their lack of culture?
> Note the branch of crepe myrtle in a blue porcelain vase.
>
> (3:32/16a)

Yang, like so many of his contemporaries, was a lover of T'ang poetry, and was particularly fond of the works of Po Chü-i and his friend Yüan Chen. He felt, however, that the poems of these two men were too much taken up with their own friendship and other private matters, and were lacking in themes of universal interest and importance. He voiced his objection in the following poem from his second collection. It is a seven-character *chüeh-chü* and bears the title, "On reading the poems in the Ch'ang-ch'ing Collections of Po and Yüan." The names Shao-fu and Wei-chih refer respectively to Po Chü-i and Yüan Chen.

> I've read all the poems of Po and Yüan;
> All my life I've valued Shao-fu and Wei-chih.
> But two or three readings and I still don't get the sense –
> Half is about their friendship, half about private affairs.
>
> (3:10/3a)

It may be of interest to note in passing that Lu Yu, in a poem written in 1205 entitled "Thinking of the Past," remarked: "People say I resemble Po Chü-i, though in fact we're not alike."

I shall conclude my discussion of Yang Wan-li with another poem from his second collection, in five-character old form and called "Relaxing in the Evening in My Study, the Wo-chih-chai." In graphic terms it deals with the kind of nameless sorrow which seems to beset all men at times, and the poet's efforts to combat it through philosophy.

> I shut the door but I can't sit down;
> Opening the window, I stand in a breath of cool.
> A grove of trees shades the bright sun;
> The ink stone on my desk gives off a jade-green glow.
> I let my hand wander over scrolls of poems,
> Softly humming three or four verses.
> The first scroll I pick up pleases me greatly,
> The second suddenly makes my spirits sink.
> Throw it aside – I can't go on reading!
> I get up and wander around the armchair.
> The ancients — they had their mountains of grief,
> But my mind is clearer than the river.
> They are no concern of mine —
> Why should I break my heart over them?
> The mood is over and instead I laugh.
> One cicada urges on the evening sun.   (3:9/9a)

Yang Wan-li's friendship with Lu Yu is mentioned in some detail in the poem entitled "Song of the Cloud Dragon" in his fifth collection, and by Lu Yu in the long poem written when he said goodby to his son Lu Tzu-lung, which we have already noted.

In addition to Lu Yu, Fan Ch'eng-ta, and Yang Wan-li, two other men, Yu Mao and Hsiao Te-tsao, are often mentioned as important poets of the time, but for some reason their works have not survived. Sung poetry of this period became widely read in Japan toward the close of the Edo period, mainly because of the efforts of the scholar Yamamoto Hokuzan (1752–1812). A selection of Lu Yu's poems, the *Riku Hōō shishō*, was published in 1801, a selection from Fan Ch'eng-ta, the *Han Sekko shishō*, in 1804, and from Yang Wan-li, the *Yō Seisai shishō*, in 1808. All contained prefaces by Yamamoto Hokuzan. This was done partly in reaction to the view, propounded a century earlier by Ogyū Sorai, that T'ang poetry alone was worthy of respect. At the same time these Sung works happened to coincide with the literary taste that is reflected in the works of the famous haiku master Buson, a contemporary of Yamamoto Hokuzan who enjoyed great popularity at this time.

A word may be added here about the great Confucian philosopher Chu Hsi (1130–1200), whose father, Chu Sung, a poet of considerable merit, has already been mentioned. First, I shall quote an example of Chu Hsi's poetry, a seven-character *chüeh-chü* entitled "Coming Down Chu-jung Peak Drunk." It was written when he was traveling through Mount Heng in Hunan, probably by palanquin.

> I've come ten thousand li, riding the long wind;
> Sheer cliffs, heaped clouds stir my heart.
> Three cups of cloudy wine and my nerve is up.
> Singing out loud, I swoop down from Chu-jung Peak.

(26:5/8b)

Here is another example, one of a group of five-character *chüeh-chü* with the collective title "Cloud Valley," the name of his country home at Wu-yi in Fukien. This particular quatrain is subtitled "Lotus Pond."

> Gleaming brightly, the marble blossoms
> Stand far off, reflected in clear green jade.
> Only I fear that in the shining of the mountain moon
> They will turn to cold dew and fall beneath its rays.

(26:6/5b)

Chu Hsi also showed great ability as a literary critic, as may be seen in the later chapters of the *Chu-tzu yü-lei* which record his remarks on literature, and in his theories of literature as they are expounded in his own writings, such as his "Letter to Kung Chung-chih." In addition, he wrote important commentaries on the *Book of Odes* and the *Ch'u-tzu*, or *Songs of Ch'u*, as well as editing the works of the T'ang scholar and poet Han Yü. He expressed particular fondness for the T'ang poets Li Po and Ch'en Tzu-ang, but did not care for the late works of Tu Fu. Among his contemporaries he awarded first place to Lu Yu. The seven-character *chüeh-chü* so often quoted in Japanese textbooks which contains the dour warning:

> Youth quickly turns to age, learning is hard;
> You cannot afford to waste a single moment!

is not found among Chu Hsi's collected works as they were compiled by his disciples. Though it may in fact have been writen by Chu Hsi, it does little to enhance his reputation as a poet.

Not only Chu Hsi, but such other important scholars of the time as Lou Yüeh, Hung Mai, the latter's older brother Hung Kua, and Chou Pi-ta, also wrote poetry that appears to have considerable interest, though I have not had the opportunity to examine it carefully. I shall simply quote here one example, a poem in seven-character regulated verse by Lou Yüeh. It is called "Remonstrating With a Man Who Grieves at Autumn," and is an excellent example of the typical Sung desire to transcend sorrow.

> Ten thousand leagues of yellow clouds gathered up in a moment:
> I delight to see the tall sky, autumn's wind and dew.
> When the seasons have come this far, they'll soon announce the end;
> When a man reaches old age, should he not go home to rest?
> I know the scenes of nature can stir our feelings;
> I also know that fools do too much grieving.
> If the mind is truly free from all snares,
> How can the autumn moon make a man sad?   (28:12/12a)

Chapter Seven

THE END OF THE

SOUTHERN SUNG

1200–1280

Poets among the Common People

The closing years of the Southern Sung — that is, the first eight decades of the thirteenth century — produced no major poet, but only a host of minor poets who wrote minor poems. Most of the period falls within the reigns of two emperors, Emperor Ning-tsung (1195–1224) and Emperor Li-tsung (1225–1264). The former ascended the throne in 1195 when his father, Emperor Kuang-tsung, retired because of family discord. Han T'o-chou, the minister who aided Emperor Ning-tsung to ascend the throne, is noted in history for having banished Chu Hsi and other members of his group, fifty-nine men in all, on the grounds that they were "hypocritical scholars." Lu Yu has often been criticized for the fact that in his late years he wrote a piece entitled "Record of the Southern Garden" that describes the garden of Han T'o-chou's house. Han launched an unsuccessful attack on the Chin and was put to death in the palace. At the request of the Chin, his head was later removed from the coffin and sent to the Chin capital at Peking. A new peace treaty was concluded with the Chin, a fact that was celebrated by a change of era name in 1208. By this time the Mongol leader, Chinggis Khaghan, had begun attacks on the Chin, which in time forced the Chin to move its capital from Peking to K'ai-feng, but the true state of affairs in the north was not clearly known to the Sung people in the Yangtze valley. In addition, the real fury of Chinggis Khaghan's assault was at this time directed toward Europe, so that the people of the Southern Sung — at least the common people — felt little concern over what was happening beyond the borders of the empire. The situation was much like that in Japan near the close of the Edo period when rumors of the black ships from the West went largely ignored.

Emperor Li-tsung, though only distantly related to his predecessor, succeeded, with the help of the statesman Shih Mi-yüan, in forcing aside the intended heir and ascending the throne in 1225. He lifted the interdict against Chu Hsi's party and paid high respect to the Neo-Confucian philosophy, known in Chinese as *li-hsüeh*, or "philosophy of reason"; he was accordingly given the posthumous name Li-tsung, or "Sovereign of Reason." Another act of his long reign was to lower the honorary rank which had been posthumously conferred upon Wang An-shih, who from this time on was regarded as an enemy of Neo-Confucianism. Shih Mi-yüan wielded great power during the first decade of his reign and persecuted those men among the common people who were rash enough to write poems criticizing him, as we shall see later. While the Sung court proclaimed a succession of cheerful and auspicious era names such as Upright Peace, Felicitous Splendor, Precious Protection, Unfolding Blessings, and so on, in the North Chinggis Khaghan's successor, Ögödei Khaghan, conquered the Chin state (whose downfall is the theme of the laments of the famous Chin poet Yüan Hao-wen). The Mongols went on to conquer the regions of Yünnan, Tibet, and Vietnam, and the fourth ruler, Mangku Khaghan, together with his brother (later Khubilai Khaghan), led his troops in attacks on Sung territory in Szechwan and Hupei. Chia Ssu-tao, the younger brother of Emperor Li-tsung's favorite concubine, succeeded in repulsing these attacks, and the court remained in the pleasure-loving city of Hangchow. The Mongols suffered at this time from internal dissension, but from the year 1260, when Khubilai Khaghan adopted the era name Chung-t'ung, or Unification of China, it was obvious where their ambitions lay.

During the ten-year reign of Emperor Li-tsung's nephew and successor, Emperor Tu-tsung, Chia Ssu-tao continued in power, living with his beloved concubines in an official residence at a place called Arrowroot Ridge overlooking West Lake in Hangchow, surrounded by followers and lackeys and spending his days watching cricket fights.

The *Millet-Dream Record*,[1] which describes the daily life of Hang-chow, was written in 1274, the last year of Emperor Tu-tsung's reign. That same year, Khubilai dispatched his armies once more against the Sung. In 1275 Chia Ssu-tao, called to account for the Chinese defeats, was banished, and later strangled to death at a small temple in Chang-chou. Early in 1276 the Mongol general Bayan marched into Hangchow and carried off the seven-year-old Sung emperor to Ta-tu, the present Peking. Wen T'ien-hsiang, Lu Hsiu-fu, and other patriots attempted to prolong the life of the dynasty by spiriting off other members of the imperial family to Fukien and Kwangtung, but their efforts were fruitless.

Preceding these events, ignorance of the true seriousness of the situation beyond its boundaries had given the people of the Yangtze Valley some seven decades of peace and tranquility extending through most of the thirteenth century. However, after Lu Yu and Yang Wan-li, both of whom died in the early years of that century, the southern region was to produce no more major poets. The important poet of the century is to be found in the north where the storm of Mongol expansion raged, in the person of Yüan Hao-wen of the Chin, the singer of laments. Also worthy of note is Yeh-lü-ch'u-ts'ai, who accompanied Chinggis Khaghan on his march of conquest to the west, and who was the first man to describe the scenes of the west through the medium of Chinese verse.[2]

But this does not mean that poetic circles in the Southern Sung were dormant. On the contrary, they were extremely active, perhaps because no great poet was on the scene, and the countless minor poets, living in their region of peace and tranquility, turned out countless minor poems. The situation resembled the burst of literary activity that marked the end of the Edo period in Japan.

Mediocre as the individual works of these minor poets may be, taken together they signal several important changes in literary development, a fact that must not be overlooked. First, we should note that the majority of them were not government officials, but private citizens,

---

[1] See above, p. 4.

[2] Both men are dealt with in the author's untranslated book on poetry of the Yüan and Ming periods, *Genminshi gaisetu*, previously noted.

some of them merchants in the cities, others provincial landlords. In preceding centuries it had been the members of the bureaucracy who were the principal producers and custodians of literature, but in the Yüan, Ming, and Ch'ing this role passed into the hands of private citizens. The first sign we have of the change appears here in the last years of the Southern Sung. If one may be permitted a rather peculiar turn of expression, it was the beginning of the democratization of literature.

The second important point to note is that, since this new poetry was written mainly by private citizens, often of rather limited education, it was difficult to maintain the high level of intellectual content that had characterized the works of the earlier poets of the Sung. Accordingly, the tendency to return to the simple lyricism of T'ang poetry is stronger than ever. The strong preference for T'ang models that marks Yüan and Ming poetry may be said to stem from this period.

True, it was not entirely unheard of before this time for private citizens to write poetry. For instance, late in the eleventh century a "poetry society" was formed in Chin-ling (Nanking) consisting of the pawnbroker Wang Fortieth, the wine dealer Wang Twenty-fourth, and the haberdasher Second Uncle Ch'en. This is related in a collection of anecdotes about poetry [3] which records the following seven-character *chüeh-chü* by the pawnbroker, entitled "Seeing a Visitor Off."

> A chaos of willow flowers surrounds the misty village;
> Thinking of the one who is leaving breaks my heart.
> I come back from the riverbank with cheerless thoughts.
> The garden full of wind and rain, of course dusk comes early.

(49:9a)

To the best of my knowledge, however, this is the only reference to citizen poets during the Northern Sung, though two centuries later they have become a well-known phenomenon. A fairly large number of the private poets of the end of the Southern Sung became the "pure guests" or clients of high officials such as Han T'o-chou or Chia Ssu-tao,

---

[3] *Ts'ang-hai shih-hua*, by one Wu K'o, whose life spanned the end of the Northern and beginning of the Southern Sung. This particular anecdote refers to the Yüan-yu reign-period (1086–1093) of Emperor Che-tsung, when Su Tung-p'o was in power as leader of the Old Laws party.

making their living by acting as advisers to these men on questions of literary or artistic taste. The high officials seem to have welcomed this state of affairs, and men like Liao Ying-chung and Huang Kung-shao were well known as "guests" or art connoisseurs in the household of Chia Ssu-tao.

The Four Lings of Yung-chia

The earliest of these citizen poets of the thirteenth century are the so-called "Four Lings of Yung-chia," who lived in the early years of the century during the reign of Emperor Ning-tsung. All were natives of Yung-chia, a city on the seacoast in Chekiang. Their names were Chao Shih-hsiu, Weng Ch'üan, Hsü Chao, and Hsü Chi, and all had literary names which included the character Ling or "supernatural." Chao Shih-hsiu and Hsü Chi at one time held official positions, but only very minor ones.

All four clearly state that the works of the T'ang period should be taken as the model for poetry. They tried in particular to imitate the elegant simplicity of middle and late T'ang works, especially those in five-character regulated verse. They believed that these were the qualities and forms most suitable for the citizen poet. As an example of their work, let me quote a poem in this form by Hsü Chi entitled "My Hut."

> The vine door shuts and opens again;
> A faraway home is best for a man of no talent.
> I transplant lotus, feeling sorry for the old plot where it grew;
> I buy stones – they come complete with new moss.
> Medicine? I trust the drugs of the immortals.
> Clothes? I follow an old fashioned cut.
> Since I never had a post to quit in the first place.
> What use do I have for a poem on "Going Home"?   (16:1a)

The last line is a reference to the famous poem, "Going Home," written by T'ao Yüan-ming when he retired from public office.

The other three poets also composed poems of this type, recording in clear, simple language the joys of the life of a commoner. Here, for example, is a poem in seven-character regulated verse by Chao Shih-hsiu. It is entitled "To thank a friend who called on me after I had moved to my new house," and probably refers to a house he rented in Hangchow.

> I've managed to rent a house – my mind feels lighter;
> This ailing body will have a place to rest from care.
> Bamboo shoots poke up through broken paving bricks;
> The hills are bright above the trees next door.
> There's a well of the sweetest water — I'll try some tea.
> No flowers to stick in it — leave the vase empty.
> I hardly know the people in alleys north and south;
> How kind — my poet friend came so far to rap at my door!
>
> (6:14a)

Turning to another form, here is an example of a seven-character *chüch-chü*. It is by Hsü Chi and is called "Sitting Doing Nothing on a Summer Day."

> Countless mountain cicadas shrill in the evening sun;
> In the shade of tall peaks I sit where shadows are cool.
> By the rock's edge I happen to see the drip of a spring;
> With the wind passing I can just catch the scent of pine needles.
>
> (16:10b)

All four men wrote poems which, as may be seen from the examples quoted, are small in scale and feeling, and yet all consciously believed that they were returning to the ideals of T'ang poetry. Hsü Chi wrote, "Poetry should take its lines from the T'ang men" (16:6b) and Hsü Chao expressed the opinion that "for poetry, you need the T'ang style and then some polishing" (18:11a). The political theorist and leader of the so-called Yung-chia Party, Yeh Shih, who also lived in Yung-chia, seems to have acted as the patron and leader of the poetic group, and he wrote grave inscriptions for Hsü Chao and Hsü Chi in which he praised the achievements of the group, declaring that "T'ang poetry is being written once again" (40:21/11b). He added that it was regrettable they did not succeed in reviving the style of the greatest period of T'ang poetry, the age of Tu Fu and Li Po.

The important thing to note, I believe, is that although the works of these minor poets are of limited interest, they deal with the joys of everyday life. These writers were consciously imitating T'ang poetry, and yet their works are not overshadowed by sorrow, a fact which reflects the influence of Su Tung-p'o and his efforts to break from the older tradition of poetic melancholy.

Chao Shih-hsiu compiled an anthology of T'ang poetry entitled *Chung-miao-chi*, or *Collection of Many Wonders*, which seems to have been used as a handbook by his fellow poets. It contains 228 poems by seventy-six poets, beginning with Shen Ch'üan-ch'i in the early T'ang and extending to Wang Chen-po in late T'ang. Over half the poems are superficial works in five-character regulated verse. The fact that no works by the greatest of the T'ang poets such as Li Po, Tu Fu, Han Yü, and Po Chü-i are included probably represents a policy of deliberately avoiding the real giants of the past.

The Chiang-hu, or River and Lake School

The next group of poets to be considered after the Four Lings is that referred to as the Chiang-hu School. The term Chiang-hu derives from *chiang-hu shih-chi*, the title of a collection of the works of one hundred and nine poets, compiled by a book-dealer of Hangchow named Ch'en Ch'i: *Chiang-hu* — "rivers and lakes" — implies that the men represented in the anthology are, like the compiler Ch'en Ch'i himself, private citizens rather than government officials. Ch'en Ch'i, too, was a poet, and his collected works, entitled *Yün-lin yi-kao*, are included in the anthology he compiled. I shall begin by quoting one of his poems, a seven-character *chüeh-chü* called "Getting Up Early."

> This morning, spirits fresh, my step feels light;
> With goosefoot cane I stroll to the end of the garden.
> Street cries – they too have something to say.
> I buy autumn flowers to stick in the little vase.
>
> (61:10a)

Ch'en Ch'i's bookshop was located in the Mu-ch'in ward of Hangchow. It is described in the following poem in five-character regulated verse by Chao Shih-hsiu, one of the "Four Lings" discussed in the previous section. In the last line Chao expresses his gratitude to the book-dealer for letting him use the reference books in his shop when his own books were destroyed by fire. Hangchow, it may be noted, was notorious for the frequency of its fires.

> Past and present surround him on four sides;
> All day long he sits in the center.
> The gate faces the public canal,
> The eaves slope in the shade of green trees.
> Often he invites famous men for a drink;
> Sometimes he asks me to write a poem.
> Since my books were all burned, I'm grateful to him
> For letting me come and look things up.   (6:10a)

As this poem indicates, Ch'en Ch'i was first of all a bookseller; but he was also active as a publisher, bringing out a series of editions of T'ang poetry, particularly of the works of minor poets, to meet the demands of his fellow poets for T'ang works. These editions are known to bibliographers as *Ch'en-shih shu-p'eng pen*, or "Editions from Mr. Ch'en's Bookstall." Another undertaking was, as we have seen, the compilation and publication of the works of his contemporaries, which he gathered together to form the *Chiang-hu shih-chi*, or *River and Lake Collection*. This work seems to have enjoyed a wide sale, and in time involved its publisher in difficulties with government authorities. Among the works included in the *River and Lake Collection* was the *Nan-yüeh-kao*, a group of poems by Liu K'o chuang, whom I shall discuss later. The poems include a seven-character regulated verse called "Fallen Plum Blossom" which was believed to express pity for Emperor Ning-tsung's adopted son Hung, the Prince of Chi, who was prevented from succeeding to the throne by the prime minister Shih Mi-yüan and died an unhppy death. The authorities, their suspicions aroused by this example of covert political comment, began to examine the other poems in the anthology. In the works of the bookseller Ch'en Ch'i they came across this suspicious couplet:

> Autumn rain on the pagoda tree – the Imperial Prince's mansion;
> Spring wind through the willows – the Prime Minister's bridge.

The works of another poet, Tseng Chi, revealed the following laconic statement:

Ninety days of spring, but clear sunlight is scarce;
In a hundred or a thousand years, how many times of trouble!

The poets were called up for investigation, the woodblocks from which the anthology had been printed were destroyed, and its publisher, Ch'en Ch'i, was banished. An account of the affair is to be found in the "plum" section of the *Ying-k'uei lü-sui* by Fang Hui, and in *chüan* 16 of the *Ch'i-tung yeh-yü* by Chou Mi, with the added comment that for a time after this event it was forbidden for ordinary persons to compose poetry. The affair took place in the early years of Emperor Li-tsung's reign when Shih Mi-yüan wielded power.

But the taste for poetry writing could not be stamped out by decrees from the authorities. Among the hundred or more poets represented in the *River and Lake Collection*, a few, such as the high officials Hung Mai and Liu K'o-chuang, and the famous composer of *tz'u* songs, Chiang K'uei, are fairly well known to us from the historical sources for the period. The vast majority, however, are minor poets whose collected works have been preserved in the anthology, but about whom little is known. This fact alone strongly suggests that most of them were simply private citizens. Two of the *River and Lake* poets, Tai Fu-ku and Liu K'o-chuang, are noteworthy for the large volume of their poetry, and I shall therefore discuss them in some detail.

Tai Fu-ku (1167–?)

Tai Fu-ku says of himself, "This wild man was born a farmer's son," in a place called Huang-yen in Chekiang. Later, however, he "threw away the hoe and went wandering in the four directions" (39:6/23b), making a living as a poet. His life was a long one, extending from 1167, early in the reign of Emperor Hsiao-tsung, to some time around 1250. The exact year of his death is unknown, but he was still in good health at the age of eighty. He writes of himself,

> Old man of seventy, hair white as snow,
> Settles among the rivers and lakes, selling poems.
>
> (39:1/19a)

As this indicates, he made his living by presenting poems to various prominent officials of the time and receiving support from them in exchange. The following poem, for example, in seven-character regulated verse, was sent to an official named Huang Tzu-mai who had invited Tai to his home in the capital.

> A peasant, how could I win fame by my poems?
> Poor as ever, I mount the donkey and race about the capital.
> White hair on half my head – my age is astounding;
> My empty fame in one day moves lords and ministers.
> Thinking of our meeting by the lakeside in the spring wind tomorrow,
> How can I bear the sound of night rain on the roof?
> Broken clouds beyond the willows filter the morning sunlight.
> I'll try listening to hidden birds who talk of the new clear spell.
>
> (39:6/2a)

Because his livelihood depended upon the success of his poems, he was naturally obliged at times to cater to the tastes of the age. For example, in the hope of gaining favor with the powerful Chia Ssu-tao, whose incompetence did much to hasten the fall of the Southern Sung, he could write:

> The world has only one Ch'iu-ho;
> In one age there can never be two Shih-p'ing's!
>
> (39:4/20b)

It is hardly necessary to add that Ch'iu-ho is the literary name of Chia Ssu-tao and Shih-p'ing that of Tai Fu-ku himself. According to the critic Fang Hui, who lived a little later, it became the fashion, from the closing years of the twelfth century on, for poets to try to win the patronage of prominent officials, from whom they sometimes received as much as a million cash in gifts. Fang Hui adds, however, that among such patron-seeking poets, Tai Fu-ku had the highest reputation for integrity.

In his late years Tai Fu-ku settled down in a little two-story house which his son had built for him. In the following poem in five-character regulated verse, he describes his delight with the house.

> Old now, I know I'm no more use;
> I've come home to a life of ease.

So many years I've slept in strange rooms,
Today I love my little house.
When I was out in the world, I hatched no great schemes;
At leisure now, I read old books.
As long as I can eat my fill,
I won't ask for anything else.   (39:2/24b)

Unlike the "Four Lings," Tai Fu-ku did not admire regulated verse to the exclusion of all other forms, but tried using old-poetry form for narrative and philosophical poems. He maintained that the poetry of "Our Dynasty" — that is, the Sung — derived from the Classics of the Confucian school and was in this respect quite different from the poetry of the T'ang, particularly that of the late T'ang. As a thinker he was hardly profound, but the following narrative poem exhibits an engaging sense of humor. In five-character old form, it was written when Tai was living in a small cottage and receiving support from the Chief of the Custom House of Fukien. It describes the arrival of a porter from the government office bearing gifts of wine and other articles. The meaning of the "round seal" in the third line is uncertain, though it may be a list of the gifts.

I walk into the little garden
When suddenly a black-robed porter appears.
In his hand he carries a round seal,
And delivers gifts from the provincial office,
Lining them up full before me;
All has been arranged with taste and care.
My neighbors crowd around to watch;
They look as though they're going to drool.
I call the boy to open a keg at once
And the neighbors and I all get drunk together.
                                                       (39:1/8a)

Liu K'o-chuang (1187–1269)

Liu K'o-chuang was a native of P'u-t'ien in Fukien. He was born twenty years after Tai Fu-ku, and at an early age became acquainted with the "Four Lings of Yung-chia." I have already mentioned how his poem "Fallen Plum Blossom," because of its political implications, got him into trouble with the authorities in the early years of Emperor Li-tsung's reign. The highest post he held was that of provincial judge of Fukien. His complete works, the *Hou-ts'un hsien-sheng ch'üan-chi* in 193 *chüan*, contains 48 *chüan* of poems, the largest number for any poet of this period. The total number of individual poems would appear to be several thousand, over half of them in regulated verse, or *chüeh-chü*, form. Liu himself asserts gloomily that, "Hard as I work, I never get beyond the poetry of the late T'ang" (20:4/17b), though in fact he occasionally manages to strike a note of originality, as in the following poem. In five-character regulated verse, it is called "Weeping for Hsüeh Tzu-shu." Chin-t'an, where Mr. Hsüeh lived, is in Kiangsu.

> When the doctor came from Chin-t'an,
> He said the disease could still be cured.
> No one believed it was serious;
> When we heard he was dead, we thought it was a lie.
> His friends are putting in order the manuscripts he left;
> His wife can read off instructions for the funeral.
> I gather up the books I had borrowed from him
> And, hiding my tears, return them to his son.   (20:1/4b)

He also wrote poems in which, as a responsible member of the government, he expressed concern over relations with the Mongols. Examples are to be found in his "Six Poems to Send to the Soldiers Guarding the Yangtze," "Song on Digging Moats," and "Song on Transporting Rations." Another is the following seven-character *chüeh-chü* entitled "Something that Happened When I Went with Cheng Chün-jui to Lai-ch'i."

> News from the north these days is scarce and hard to trust;
> Along the road the call to arms may go out at any time.
> I'm grieved to look in the mirror at a head gone grey,
> Ashamed to look at the government's recruiting flags hung out.
>   (20:7/14b)

In his late years he retired to the countryside, and many of the poems from this period deal with his relations with the local farmers. Here is an example in seven-character *chüeh-chü* form called "Leaving the City."

> I stop for a rest at the wine seller's west of the city;
> Where the green shade is deepest, crows are cawing.
> The proprietor sighs – Sir, you have come too late:
> All gone – the blossoms on the trellis of flowering thorn.
>
> (20:5/17b)

It would seem that life in retirement was not always easy, as shown by the following poem, one of a series entitled "Ten Poems Recording Things that Happened at the Year's End." In seven-character *chüeh-chü* form, it tells how Liu was forced by his own poverty to turn a beggar away from his door.

> A beggar in patched robe stands by my door;
> How would he know I'm hard put to get through the years remaining?
> The dyer, the wine woman – I owe them money still,
> And on top of that I must send my boy money for his school.
>
> (20:3/5a)

Retired officials living on government pensions were obliged to pay taxes like ordinary property owners, a hardship which Lu Yu complains about in his poetry; and judging from the poem quoted above, Liu K'o-chuang found life difficult for the same reason. Liu also wrote on other features of country life, such as the village school, or the local theatrical performances; with this interest in farm life, he might be called a minor Lu Yu. He died at the age of eighty-three in 1269, seven years before the fall of Hangchow.

Another poet-official of this period, who advanced as high as the post of secretary of the Civil Board, was Fang Yüeh (1198–1262).[4] Fang Yüeh was the son of a farm family in Hsin-an in Anhwei, and later in life expressed regret that he had ever left home to become an official, as in the following poem in five-character old form.

> Once I was a man who worked the fields;
> I could count the number of characters I knew.

[4] An edition of Fang's works was published in Japan in 1805 by Ōkubo Shibutsu, who wrote poetry in Chinese and worked to introduce Sung poetry to Japan.

Who made me sit by the lamp at the little window
And stole from me the plowing-time rains?   (7:6a)

In keeping with his humble background, Fang Yüeh's poems have a
plebeian tone, and include such pieces as one written to present to the
bookbinder. Among his works are ten poems in five-character lines called
"T'ang Style Regulated Verse." This title was also used by other poets
as well, and indicates the love for T'ang poetry among the men of these
times. Fang also wrote a poem satirizing the man who, bearing a name
card which proclaims him an expert in "lute playing, chess, calligraphy,
and painting," goes about visiting one after another of the prominent
officials (7:20b). We are reminded again of the prevalence of poets and
connoisseurs who lived on the patronage of wealthy officials at this
time.

The *San-t'i-shih, Shih-jen yü-hsieh,* and *Ts'ang-lang shih-hua*

As we have seen, the atmosphere of the last decades of the Southern
Sung closely resembled that of Japan in the late Edo period. In an aura
of peace, oblivious to the crisis which was drawing near, the poetry
groups of the thirteenth century — made up principally of private citizens rather than officials — worked to develop their poetic theories,
giving clear articulation to the fondness for T'ang poetry that had been
an underlying current of taste since the beginning of the Southern Sung.
But the T'ang poetry which these men admired and strove to imitate was
the relatively light-hearted verse of the latter years of that dynasty, the
so-called Middle and Late T'ang.

The anthology of T'ang poetry known as *San-t'i-shih,* or *San-t'i T'ang-
shih — T'ang Poems in Three Forms —* which has been so popular in
Japan since it was first introduced by the Zen monks in late Kamakura
times — was compiled at this time by Chou Pi, one of the *River and
Lake* poets of the reign of Emperor Li-tsung. The anthology consists of
poems in seven-character *chüeh-chü* form, and in seven-character and
five-character regulated verse, taken from works of middle and late T'ang
writers. The compiler distinguishes two kinds of poetic lines, the *hsü*

— "felt" or lyric line; and the *shih* — "actual" or scene-description line. He then distinguishes the ways in which various poems make use of these two types of lines — two lines describing scenery followed by two lines expressing emotion; the reverse of this, or four lines devoted entirely to description or to emotion — and arranges the selections accordingly. The anthology seems to have been intended as a kind of handbook for amateur poets and suggests that there must have been an increasing demand for books of this type. The critic Fang Hui (1227–1306), who lived a little later, employs in his *Ying-k'uei lü-sui* a terminology which is derived from that of the *San-t'i-shih*, his *ch'ing*, or "feeling," being equivalent to Chou Pi's *hsü*, or "felt," and his *ching*, or "scenery," being equivalent to Chou Pi's *shih*, or "actual."

Another type of book concerned with poetry that became very popular at this time was the *shih-hua*, or "remarks on poetry." In the early days of the Northern Sung, Ou-yang Hsiu had put together his remarks concerning poetry under the title *Shih-hua*, and in the following centuries books of this kind, made up of anecdotes and critical remarks, became so numerous that someone was led to observe that "when the 'remarks on poetry' came into fashion, poetry died." By the early years of the Southern Sung two large encyclopedias based upon such works had already been published, the *T'iao-ch'i yü-yin ts'ung-hua* (*Anthology of Remarks on Poetry by the Fisherman-Hermit of T'iao-ch'i*), and the *Shih-hua tsung-kuei* (*A Master Key to the Remarks on Poetry*), to be followed in the thirteenth century by the best of the *shih-hua* genre, the *Shih-jen yü-hsieh* — *Jade Chips from the Poets* (preface dated 1244). This last is noteworthy not only for its contents, but also for the fact that it was clearly printed as a commercial venture. Commercial printing had already begun to appear in the Northern Sung, though the vast majority of books printed were government-sponsored editions. By the thirteenth century, as we have already seen in the case of the book-dealer and publisher Ch'en Ch'i, printing was becoming a profitable commercial enterprise, and one after another of the private editions called *fang-k'o-pen*, or "city editions," were published. Such works, needless to say, could not help but fan the enthusiasm of the common citizens for literature.

The belief that in studying T'ang poetry one should not study just any phase that took one's fancy, but should seek out and imitate its finest products — an isolated opinion at the time — finds expression in the *Ts'ang-lang shih-hua* of Yen Yü. Yen Yü was a friend of Tai Fu-ku and appears, like him, to have been a private citizen. Tai Fu-ku's poems indicate that the two men exchanged opinions on poetry. Yen Yü's views borrowed the terminology of Ch'an (Zen) Buddhism, and may be summed up as follows: Li Po, Tu Fu, and the other poets of the High T'ang period, along with the poets of the earlier Han, Wei, and Chin dynasties, attained what in Zen terms may be called the highest level of enlightenment. In contrast to these, Han Yü, Po Chü-i, and the other poets of the middle T'ang achieved only the secondary level, that of Hinayana, or "Lesser Vehicle" Zen. And when it comes to the poets of the late T'ang, he declares severely, they are on the lowest level (that of the *śrāvaka pratyeka*). Accordingly the so-called "T'ang style" which Chao Shih-hsiu, Weng Ch'üan, and the other poets of the *River and Lake* school imitate, being that of the late T'ang poets such as Chia Tao and Yao Ho, is far from the highest level. The custom of dividing the history of T'ang poetry into four periods, Early, High, Middle, and Late, and of regarding the High T'ang period as the apex, began with Yen Yü and became accepted practice from Ming times on.

In comparing T'ang poetry with that of "the present dynasty" — that is, the Sung — Yen Yü remarks that "without even discussing the question of skill, one notices immediately that they are not the same in feeling." "The poems of the High T'ang period," he states, "are like sounds in the air, colors in a form, the moon in the water, or the shapes in a mirror; though the words come to an end, the meaning is never exhausted." By contrast, men of recent times "make poetry out of prose, out of pedantry, or out of argument."

A fondness for the poetry of the late T'ang had led the men of Yen Yü's time to a new appreciation of T'ang poetry as a whole, and Yen Yü's theories were an attempt to direct attention to the periods and qualities that are the core of its excellence, though it was not until the Ming that his poetic theories were put into actual practice. In expressing dissatisfaction with the poetry of "the present dynasty," Yen Yü reminds us that by his day Sung poetry, along with the Sung political regime, was faltering to its end.

Wen T'ien-hsiang (1236–1282), Poet of Resistance

The poetry of the Southern Sung, which seemed as though it might continue indefinitely with the murmurings of countless minor poets, at the very last detonated in a blaze of passion. The event which brought this about could only be called the natural and inevitable result of the international situation, and yet it was an event which to the Sung people, at least to the ordinary citizens of Hangchow and the other cities, came as an utter surprise. I refer, of course, to the Mongol invasion, by which the Sung dynasty was brought to an end. The outburst of passion which it occasioned found its most eloquent expression in the poems of the man who was the last prime minister of the doomed regime and the leader of the resistance movement after the downfall of the Sung, Wen T'ien-hsiang (1236–1282), who died a prisoner of the Mongols in Peking. Particularly famous is his Cheng-ch'i-ko, or "Song of the Upright Spirit." But the history of Wen T'ien-hsiang's life is so closely interwoven with that of the Mongol invasion that I shall defer a detailed discussion of his art to the section on the poetry of the Yüan which will appear in the succeeding volume of this series.[5]

---

[5] Kōjirō Yoshikawa, *Genminshi gaisetsu (Introduction to Yüan and Ming Poetry)*. This book was published in Tokyo in 1963, but has not been translated into English [Tr.].

FINDING LIST

FINDING LIST

List of Abbreviations

CHSKCNPCS   *Ch'üan Han San-kuo Chin Nan-pei-ch'ao shih*, 3 vols. (Taipei 1962)
SPPY   *Ssu-pu pei-yao*
SPTK   *Ssu-pu ts'ung-k'an*
SSC   *Sung-shih-ch'ao* (1914)
TSCC   *Ts'ung-shu chi-ch'eng*

Chinese Works Cited

Poems and other quoted material in the text are taken from the works listed below. In the reference numbers inserted in the text, the first number refers to the work as it is found in this list. The second number refers to the *chüan*, and the third to the page; in works that do not exceed one *chüan* in length, only the page number is given. References to the *Ch'üan T'ang-shih* (No. 14) are to the continuous page numbers. Brief descriptions of the works have been added after the titles.

1. *An-yang chi-ch'ao* (poetry of Han Ch'i), in SSC.
2. *Ch'a-shan-chi* (poetry of Tseng Chi), in TSCC.
3. *Ch'eng-chai-chi* (poetry of Yang Wan-li), in SPTK.
4. *Chien-nan shih-kao* (poetry of Lu Yu), in SPPY.
5. *Ch'ing-hsiang tsa-chi* (anecdotes on early Sung history by Wu Ch'u-hou), in *Pai-hai*.
6. *Ch'ing-yüan-chai-chi* (poetry of Chao Shih-hsiu), in SSC.
7. *Ch'iu-ya hsiao-kao-ch'ao* (poetry of Fang Yüeh), in SSC.
8. *Chu-p'o shih-hua* (remarks on poetry by Chou Tzu-chih), in TSCC.
9. *Chu-tzu ta-ch'üan* (works of Chu Hsi), in SPPY.
10. *Chü-tz'u chi-ch'ao* (poetry of Ch'ao Ch'ung-chih), in SSC.
11. *Ch'üan Chin-shih* (*Complete Chin Poetry*), in CHSKCNPCS.

12. *Ch'üan Han-shih* (*Complete Han Poetry*), in CHSKCNPCS.
13. *Ch'üan San-kuo-shih* (*Complete Three Kingdoms Poetry*), in CHSKCNPCS.
14. *Ch'üan T'ang-shih* (*Complete T'ang Poetry*), 12 vols. (Peking 1960).
15. *Chung-min-kung shih-chi* (poetry of K'ou Chun), in SPTK.
16. *Erh-wei-t'ing-chi pu-ch'ao* (poetry of Hsü Chi) in *Sung-shih-ch'ao-pu* (Shanghai 1914).
17. *Fan Wen-cheng-kung chi* (poetry of Fan Chung-yen), in SPTK.
18. *Fang-lan-hsüan shih-chi* (poetry of Hsü Chao), in SSC.
19. *Hou-shan shih-chu* (poetry of Ch'en Shih-tao), in SPTK.
20. *Hou-ts'un hsien-sheng ta-ch'üan-chi* (writings of Liu K'o-chuang), in SPTK.
21. *Hsi-k'un ch'ou-ch'ang chi* (anthology of early Sung poetry), in SPTK.
22. *Hsiang-shan yeh-lu* (essays of Wen-ying), in *Ku-shu ts'ung-k'an* (1922).
23. *Hsiao-ch'u-chi* (poetry of Wang Yü-ch'eng), in SPTK.
24. *Hsiao-yao-chi* (poetry of P'an Lang), in *Chih-pu-tsu-chai ts'ung-shu* (1776).
25. *Huai-hai-chi* (poetry of Ch'in Kuan), in SPTK.
26. *Hui-an hsien-sheng Chu Wen-kung wen-chi* (writings of Chu Hsi), in SPTK.
27. *K'un-hsüeh chi-wen* (writings of Wang Ying-lin), in SPTK.
28. *Kung-k'uei-chi* (poetry of Lou Yüeh), in SPTK.
29. *Lao-hsüeh-an pi-chi* (writings of Lu Yu), in TSCC.
30. *Li Ho-ching hsien-sheng chi* (poetry of Lin Pu), in SPTK.
31. *Lin-ch'uan hsien-sheng wen-chi* (writings of Wang An-shih), in SPTK.
32. *Luan-ch'eng-chi* (poetry of Su Ch'e), in SPTK.
33. *Meng-ch'i pi-t'an* (essays by Shen K'uo), in SPTK.
34. *Nan-yang chi-ch'ao* (poetry of Han Wei), in SSC.
35. *Ou-yang Wen-chung-kung chi* (poetry of Ou-yang Hsiu), in SPTK.
36. *Shan-fang sui-pi* (writings of Chiang Tzu-cheng), in *Chih-pu-tsu-chai ts'ung-shu*.
37. *Shan-ku-shih chi-chu* (annotated poetry of Huang T'ing-chien), in SPPY.
38. *Shih-hu chü-shih shih-chi* (poetry of Fan Ch'eng-ta), in SPTK.
39. *Shih-ping shih-chi* (poetry of Tai Fu-ku), in SPTK, 2nd ser.
40. *Shui-hsin hsien-sheng wen-chi* (writings of Yeh Shih), in SPTK.
41. *Shui-yün shih-ch'ao* (poetry of Wang Yüan-liang), in SSC.
42. *Su Hsüeh-shih wen-chi* (writings of Su Shun-ch'in), in SPTK.

43. *Su Wen-chung-kung shih-ho-chu* (poetry of Su Tung-p'o, annotated by Feng Ying-liu), 1793.
44. *Sung chiu-kung-jen shih-tz'u* (poems by former palace ladies of Sung), in TSCC.
45. *Sung-shih chi-shih* (*Notes on Sung Poetry*), 1736–1795.
46. *T'an-yüan-chi* (poetry of Wen T'ung), in SPTK.
47. *T'iao-ch'i yü-yin ts'ung-hua* (anthology of remarks on poetry), in SPPY.
48. *Ts'an-liao-tzu shih-chi* (poetry of Ts'an-liao), in SPTK.
49. *Ts'ang-hai shih-hua* (anthology of remarks on poetry by Wu K'o), in *Shuang-wu-hsüan ssu-chung* 2 (1841).
50. *Tseng-kuang chien-chu Chien-chai shih-chi* (annotated poetry of Ch'en Yü-yi), in SPTK.
51. *Tung-kuan-chi* (poetry of Wei Yeh), in *Sung pai-chia shih-ts'un* (1741).
52. *Tung-p'o t'i-pa* (prefaces and postfaces by Su Tung-p'o), in *Ching-tai pi-shu* (1630).
53. *Wan-ling hsien-sheng chi* (poetry of Mei Yao-ch'en), in SPTK.
54. *Wang Ching-kung nien-p'u k'ao-lüeh* (chronology of the life of Wang An-shih), Ts'ai Shang-hsiang (Peking 1959).
55. *Wang Ching-wen-kung shih chien-chu* (annotated poetry of Wang An-shih), Peking 1958.
56. *Wei-chai-chi* (poetry of Chu Sung), in SPTK, 2nd ser.
57. *Yi-ch'uan chi-jang chi* (poetry of Shao Yung), in SPTK.
58. *Ying-k'uei lü-sui* (critical remarks by Fang Hui), 1712.
59. *Yü-chang Huang hsien-sheng wen-chi* (writings of Huang T'ing-chien), in SPTK.
60. *Yü-hsüan Sung-shih* (*Imperial Anthology of Sung Poetry*) in *Yü-hsüan Sung Chin Yüan ssu-ch'ao shih* (1708).
61. *Yün-chü yi-kao* (writings of Ch'en Ch'i), in *Nan-Sung ch'ün-hsien hsiao-chi* 24 (1801).